AN UNDERSTANDING OF THE LORD'S PRAYER

by Dr. C

PRESS

AN UNDERSTANDING OF THE LORD'S PRAYER
by Dr. C

Printed in the United States of America

ISBN 9781609573263

www.xulonpress.com

to us

Contents

Introduction

Thoughts about the Lord's Prayer and its meaning have been with me for a long time. The inspiration and the setting to write about it came as my wife, Florence, and I drove across the United States. Most of the writing took place as we followed and camped along the Lewis and Clark Trail during 2006, the bicentennial year of their return east from the Pacific Ocean.

To convey the spirit of our journey I am including a section of a letter Florence wrote to friends and family.

"Following their (Lewis' and Clark's) trail we traveled along the Columbia River through Oregon, the Snake and Clearwater Rivers through

Washington and Idaho, the Yellowstone River through Montana, the Missouri River through North and South Dakota, Iowa, Nebraska, Kansas and Missouri, then the Mississippi River to St. Louis and Cairo, Illinois where we traveled along the Ohio River into Paducah, Kentucky, the end of our "L&C" Journey. As we traveled through the Bitterroot Mountains, over the Continental Divide, through the buttes and badlands of Montana and the high treeless plains of the Dakotas we saw our country's diverse, awesome landscape. It's amazing to me that in all these places: forested or treeless, high or low, rugged or fertile, big or tiny, people like us live: speaking our common language, eating at McDonalds or Red Lobster, shopping at Kmart, Walgreens, or Sears, worshipping at their churches. We are fortunate to live in such a diverse and welcoming land."

My writing about the Lord's Prayer also conveys the spirit of a long journey. Some words given to us about 2,000 years ago continue to be said by millions of people all over the world. They must resonate with something to say, with something of value. Often these words are repeated quickly then sealed with amen and moving on to the next agenda. This book offers a pause: a pause to study, reflect, and listen to what these words given as the Lord's Prayer are saying to us.

The Prayer's historical significance is looked at and its format described. The section prayers that form the complete Word are defined and their relevance in this day and age is shown. The book explains how the insights, guidelines, and main message of the Prayer have been given to us and why. Although received as a prayer, the Lord's Prayer is meant to be lived. A chapter is devoted to living the Prayer.

As we delve into interpreting the Lord's Prayer, insights into the essence of its Author and our relationship to this Author are revealed. Why say the Prayer? How does it help us? Why was it given to us? All are questions discussed throughout the book.

Every word in the Lord's Prayer is choice and pertinent to its meaning. In the book every word is defined and its contribution to building the complete prayer is looked at. Written in a clear, concise manner the text invites and encourages the readers to think about the Prayer and put their own individual grasp on understanding it.

The book is titled "An Understanding Of The Lord's Prayer" because it expresses an understanding that I have come to after years of praying the Prayer, meditating on it, discussing it, and listening for insights from it. The book is merely sharing this understanding. I do not advocate for any particular religion. The Lord's Prayer was given to all humanity.

I thank my wife, Florence, who made the journey with me and did the word processing. I wrote; she typed. Together we put it together

Chapter 1

The Lord's Prayer

According to the Biblical record, Jesus Christ gave us the Lord's Prayer about 2,000 years ago. It has had many translations and some alterations but the initial and basic message remains the same.

A version that is currently said is:

Our Father who art in heaven,

hallowed be Thy name,

Thy kingdom come, Thy will be done

on earth as it is in heaven.

Give us this day our daily bread,

and forgive us our trespasses

as we forgive those who trespass against us.

> And lead us not into temptation
> but deliver us from evil.

Substituting the word Your for Thy is a modern version of the prayer. Its meaning is the same.

The root of the Lord's Prayer is Jewish. Jesus was a practicing Jew, fully aware of scripture and the stories of the Bible. He observed the Jewish holidays, taught in synagogues and in the Temple at Jerusalem, and was termed Rabbi which means teacher. He presented the Prayer to Jewish people. His apostles were all Jews.

As originally taught, the Lord's Prayer described the one Jewish God and embodied the meaning of Passover and the story of Exodus – the journey of the Israelites out of Egypt. See the following correlations: "Our Father" – the one true God, the God who is. "Hallowed be Thy Name" –the Lord (Yahweh) as revered in the ancient Tabernacle and in the Temple at Jerusalem, the Holy of Holies. "Thy kingdom come" – the Promised Land. "Thy will be done" – the Ten Commandments. "Give us this day our daily bread – the unleavened bread of Passover, the daily manna from heaven. "Forgive us our trespasses" – offerings, atonement. "Lead us not into temptation" – the rituals and ways of the surrounding pagans. "Deliver us from evil" – the deliverance from the false gods and tyranny of ancient Egypt.

The Jewish people who heard the Lord's Prayer were not predisposed to conceptualizing it as a Christian prayer; there was no Christian church at that time. It was a Jewish prayer and in it they would not only recognize its correlation with Exodus but would see and understand the foundation of their religion.

As the Prayer is said try to visualize the forty years journey of the Israelites, through the barren unknown, trusting in their one God: to lead them to the Promised Land, to sustain them on the way, and to protect them from temptation and evil.

The Lord's Prayer is also a documentary on the life of Jesus. He referred to God as Father and promoted the concept of the one God as his Father and our Father. Jesus fulfilled the words "Thy kingdom come, Thy will be done" by his testimony of faith and doing God's will on earth.

When agonizing and fearful of his impending harsh death, he stated not his will but God's will be done. After being tempted in the desert, Jesus knew what "lead us not into temptation" meant. He always gave thanks for his daily bread whether it be loaves of bread, fishes, or a banquet.

Like the Israelites, Jesus was delivered from evil when his family fled to Egypt after his birth and then came out of Egypt. The life of Jesus and the story of the Israelites merge within and throughout the Lord's Prayer.

Although the Lord's Prayer connects back to the faith and hope of the Israelites wandering in the desert, it is as relevant to us now as it was to them. We are all journeying through life, seeking our daily bread, looking for a heaven on earth, and tempted by false gods that surround us. It also tells our story.

The Lord's Prayer is timeless extending through history to this day. Bridging back through the Old and New Testaments and forward to our present, the Prayer becomes a pivot point between Judaism and Christianity; a position verified by the fact that Jesus was Jewish. He never stopped being a Jew. Judaism was his religion up to his death. After he died his followers were later called Christians.

Jesus stood between the faith of his Jewish forefathers and the faith of his Christian followers. It then correlates that his prayer, the Lord's Prayer, stands as the expressed transition from Judaism to Christianity. Its message was meant for people throughout all ages.

The Lord's Prayer is composed of four section prayers.

The first section prayer, "Our Father who art in heaven, hallowed be Thy name," acknowledges a God and defines our relationship to this God and to each other.

The second prayer, "Thy kingdom come, Thy will be done on earth as it is in heaven," informs us that God has a will and a purpose for us.

The third prayer, "Forgive us our trespasses as we forgive those who trespass against us," emphasizes forgiveness and shows us a way to do God's will.

The fourth prayer, "Give us this day our daily bread and lead us not into temptation but deliver us from evil," tells us what God can do for us.

These four separate section prayers form the Lord's Prayer, which throughout the book is also referred to as the Prayer. As we examine each section prayer in the following chapters, we will see how they relate to and compliment each other in formulating the complete prayer and how they lead to and reveal its major theme.

Parts of the book will be new, parts will be familiar and obvious, parts will be mystical and thought provoking. Such is life and the Lord's Prayer is a prayer about life.

Chapter 2

Our Father

The initial two words of the Lord's Prayer, "Our Father," tell us first that there is a God and acknowledge this God as the creator of all people, living and dead. The Prayer does not begin My Father, His Father, Her Father, or Their Father. The words "Our" and "Father" inform that under this God we are all connected right from the beginning: from the beginning of our existence and from the beginning of the Prayer. The value of being connected as a human family will become apparent as we proceed through the book.

Our connection to God can be mystifying, difficult to comprehend, seemingly remote; however, by putting this relationship into a familiar term

– father, we are given a concept and image that we know and understand. Many religions have used the father concept for their God in terms familiar to the existence of their members. Think about what the word father means and then extract from it the essentials of a good father; since the God in the Lord's Prayer is all good, as we will discover further on.

The good father loves his family and by love he wills and acts for their good and their well-being. He provides a home for his family, a safe and secure place. He feeds his family. He spends time with his family. He teaches them and shows them the beauty of the world around them. He allows his family members to develop their free wills and their creativity. He guides his family to do right and avoid what is wrong. He sets limits for his family for their safely and health of mind and body. He comforts them in time of pain and need; and he remains present to his family all his life. When we think of the good father we are seeing the God of the Lord's Prayer and when an earthly father does the above for his family he is showing them this God.

Now, what about the good mother? Reread the preceding paragraph describing the good father and substitute the word mother for father and she for he. When our earthly mother does the above for her family she is also showing them God. The wife and mother is a helpmate to the husband and father. In God's scheme they work together. Both reflect the image of God in their good works.

God has been termed the Power, the Creator, the Almighty, the Beginning: all useful concepts that we can define. Terming God as a father embodies the above descriptions and humanizes God bringing God closer to us, closer to home. These words, "Our Father", bring God from way out there into our realm and into our being. They connect us to God.

"Our Father" also sets the way we should view other members of the human race: as related brothers, sisters, mothers, and earthly fathers: a total human family created under God. We all have inherited the earth, we all share existence, and we all come to the same end. Most important we all have human nature with its potential to know and accept God as our Father.

I use the concept of God as a father because that is the initial image given to us in the Lord's Prayer: given to help us with our understanding and need. Although God's works are shown through male and female, I do not refer to God as a He or She, masculine or feminine – earthly terms. I refer to God as God, and as we read on, the Lord's Prayer will reveal the essence of this God to us.

Besides relating to God through the concept of a good father we can see our connection to God in the reality of our existence. Each of us can say, "I am." The dictionary definition of create is: to bring into being.[1] The fact that we do exist shows that we are created. Whether we were brought into being from evolution or out of the dust of the earth or both really makes no difference since the result is what matters: our creation, our being, our presence. Everything around us has been created: our home, the chair we sit in, the wood to build our home and chair, the tree that provided the wood. All that exits has been brought into being.

Why has God created us? A good question to ponder. Everything on earth seems to have a purpose. For example, look at trees: their leaves give us oxygen which we need to stay alive, they absorb carbon dioxide which can pollute the air, they provide food and shelter and give us the beauty of autumn foliage. Think of all the uses of wood. Think of all the purposes for water, air, soil, plants, animals. Take a mosquito: its larvae feed juvenile fish, it becomes food for swallows and bats, it forces us to develop medicines for improved health. Take the decomposers, bacteria and fungi, without which the earth would be filled with litter and necessary elements and nutrients would not be recycled. If there is purpose in life forms on earth should we be different?

To begin to understand our purpose we have to look at what we are. We are brought into being as men and women with the ability to create other men and women: a God given function to be fathers and mothers. That the means to making babies gives intense pleasure insures that babies will be created. That parents have been given the instincts and judgment to protect and provide for their offspring tells us that God wants us to continue creating and caring for the human race. When parents do not or cannot care for their children God has given others and society the means to do so. People who have children continue the being and quality of the human race. People who do not have children continue the quality of the human race. Both are equally important. The Lord's Prayer speaks indirectly to having children but directly to the quality of humanity.

But why is it of value to continue the creation of the human race? Well, for one example, the human race has given us Jesus, Gandhi, M.L. King, Lincoln, Einstein, Edison to name just a very few individuals who have helped humanity. It has given us artists, writers, musicians, sports figures, government leaders whose names you can apply. It has given us Mother Teresa and all those who care for the poor and sick. It has given us everyone both known and unknown who has helped another human being. It has given us you and me. I am sure you can think of other reasons why continuing the human race is of value.

So far men and women are the only creatures on earth who can conceptualize and verbalize that there is a God: a Creator who is termed "Our Father." We are the only form of life who can contemplate this God and give thanks for the creation of ourselves and the world around us.

We have been given the capability to study and understand the created world. Through science and individual experience we come not only to know our world but to see a plan and purpose in it. When the first human being gave thanks to God for creation an intelligent design was recognized. This intelligence has continued to be revealed to us since. An ordinary but profound example of intelligent design is light. Light travels at the incredible speed of 11,176,920 miles per minute in order to traverse long distances insuring that it reaches us from the sun, 92,960,000 miles from earth, in about 8 minutes. We, with plants, need to receive this transmitted sunlight to survive. Sound, which is less necessary for survival, travels at 12 miles per minute and just far enough for our hearing. Loud sounds, like an explosion, auto crash, or lightening, travel further to alert us to possible danger.

White light is composed of a spectrum of beautiful colors. The retinas in our eyes are able to discern this array of color. We could still exist seeing the world in shades of black and white, which animals like deer do. But, think about why we are able to see the varying and beautiful colors around us, in any part of the world, in any season. In a paint store look at all the shades of color that can be enjoyed in a home. In an art painting look at just the color. Look at flowers and think about what would be lacking if our vision were only in shades of gray. Edible fruit turns pleasant colors of orange, yellow, red, or blue, indicating it is ripe to be eaten. Think about the strawberry. Think about the blueberry. Think about why such useful colors.

Through utilizing color emissions and spectroscopy we have been able to identify elements and compounds that comprise our earth, our solar system, and outer space. The use of color indicators in laboratories, such as staining techniques to identify pathogenic bacteria, have been important in the advance of medicine. These are just a few ways color is useful to us. Much, much, more could be written about the value of this unique gift. Color, in its spectacular and wide array, exists with a purpose; it did not come to us randomly.

What applies to visualizing color applies to all our senses. Think of the purpose of hearing, of taste, of touch. Meditating on any of the senses is a path towards appreciating God's work.

When the moon rocks were analyzed, they were composed of substances like silica, which is what glass is made of: the best material for a great light reflector in the sky. On a clear night the soft moon glow is nether too bright or too dim. It's just right. Is this coincidence? The moon is just far enough from earth to prevent it from being pulled into earth's gravity and colliding with us; yet its orbit is at a distance so that its gravity can give us tides. Is this coincidence? Without tides to form currents that move ocean waters we would not have little neck clams, scallops, blue crabs, oysters, and inshore fish.

Our kidneys and liver are designed to filter waste products and toxins from our blood aiding in their excretion from our body. If they fail in their functioning we either die or obtain help from renal dialysis or a liver transplant. Intelligence permeates all life: plants turn toward light, animals hide their food, birds feed their young, man designs life saving machines and surgical operations, God designs man and woman.

Knowing our world has given us foods, medicine, technology, and conveniences; however, with this knowledge we inherit an equally important responsibility – to use our capabilities to care for and manage our God given resources. If we are given the purpose to create new life, we are also given the means to provide for and sustain this new life; which includes caring for the world that sustains us and safeguarding it for the benefit of future generations.

God also gave us the ability and freedom to enjoy our world: to swim in its waters, to ski its mountains, to view its colorful sunsets, to taste its delicious foods, to feel the warmth of sunlight, the coolness of a breeze. The list goes on and on and we can add to the list our own personal enjoyments.

In summary: we have been created to continue and care for the human race – our brothers and sisters, to know God, to give thanks to God for creation, and to know, manage, and enjoy the world we live in. Caring for the human race includes carrying out God's will on earth which will be defined in subsequent chapters.

So two words, "Our" and "Father," identify God like a loving father, define who we are in relation to God, and imply why we were created.

Chapter 3

Who Art In Heaven

M ankind has projected various descriptions of heaven: a pearly gate in the clouds, a happy hunting ground, a paradise where virgins wait in tents. The Lord's Prayer simply specifies that heaven is where God is; clearly stated, heaven is where God is. Based on this statement and the second reference in the prayer, "Thy will be done on earth as it is in heaven," we can try to derive a concept of this heaven: the heaven of the Lord's Prayer.

In the Prayer, a location for heaven is not identified except to say it is where God is. This opens the possibility that it may not only be a place or something out there, elsewhere, but it may exist here on earth. If so, this heaven could be a condition or state of existence. It could even be within us. It could exist as a whole or part of a whole, as a transition through and from life on earth, as a continuum, a parting, an ending, or as another beginning.

Traditionally we have looked up to a heaven above us, above the skies and beyond, a place where our souls can rise to and it may well be. However, if there is a possibility that heaven can exist on earth and within us then we can say that God can exist on earth and within us since heaven is where God is. Conversely if we first believe that God can exist on earth and within us then we further support the concept of a heaven existing within us. Heaven is where God is.

If heaven or aspects of heaven can be experienced while living on earth how would we recognize it; how could we achieve it? The reference, "Thy will be done on earth as it is in heaven," is the starting point. By stating that there is a will of God existing in heaven and that this same will can be done on earth, the will of God becomes the link to our understanding and achieving heaven.

The will of God is defined in Chapter 5. However, just knowing this will sheds limited light on what heaven is. Thinking about the doing of the will of the God of the Lord's Prayer, and the magnitude of its effects, impacts, and results, is what leads to learning what a heaven on earth could be. Doing the will of this God is participating in bringing heaven to earth.

Since the Lord's Prayer says that God is in heaven, understanding God should give more insight into what this heaven is like. As we proceed thoughtfully through the chapters to follow, attributes of God will come into focus. We have already been introduced to God as our good Father, our Creator. By thinking on these descriptive concepts and discerning the essence of the True God, as derived in Chapter 9, more aspects of heaven will be revealed.

To conceptualize a God as the Father of creation, in all its splendor, complexity, diversity, and reality, is to begin to see a heaven around us.

Heaven is where God is. The sea, the clear blue sky, the glowing sunset, are aspects of heaven when they reflect the Creator. A loving father and mother is an aspect of heaven, the act of reproduction and the creation of a newborn are aspects of heaven, a safe, secure home is an aspect of heaven.

Much of God's creation is seen, much is unseen, much more is probably behind the scenes. The unseen, the unknown, the silence, may also help with an awareness of what heaven is. I have heard it said that silence is the language of God and that silence speaks if we listen to it. Try to listen to what a flower or a tree has to say. Seeing and appreciating the Creator is the key to the door of heaven; doing the will of God opens this door on earth.

If heaven is reflected in creation, shown through doing the will of God, and expressed in the essence of God, then it is all around us. But we really have to look for it and look at it to make it apparent. To see a heaven on earth requires effort: an effort of seeking, looking, conceptu- alizing, and appreciating; an effort of staying focused. Saying the Lord's Prayer will help; adding your own thoughts on ways of finding heaven will also help.

So heaven, a seemingly complex abstract considered as something out there and beyond, becomes less of a mystery when looked at through the Lord's Prayer. It gains definition on earth and boundaries in the here and now. The kingdom of heaven could truly be at hand, if we grasp it.

In summary, the Prayer informs us that heaven is where God is and that we can gain an awareness of this heaven through knowing God. It also gives us an important message which is: to attain the kingdom of heaven, do the will of God while alive on earth.

Chapter 4

Hallowed Be Thy Name

Hallowed means to honor as holy, to hold in religious respect. Holy means spiritually and morally perfect or all good. The words, "hallowed be Thy name," define God as an all-good God and at the same time give due reverence and respect to this understanding of perfection.

Notice in the Lord's Prayer that no specific name for God is given. The Prayer aims to show us a conceptual god, to give us a working definition of a god for our understanding and personal use. A name is unnecessary, is a distraction, and could be misused. For example: to kill in the name of a god.

"Thy name," given as singular not plural, reveals God as a one God. Acknowledging this one God as a true God, meaning a God who is not a false god, sets the foundation for truth and truth sets the foundation for knowing what is. The importance of knowing truth for our good and for God's design for our existence is emphasized by our being given the first commandment of truth: "I am the Lord your God. You shall not have strange gods before me."

Throughout human history what have been some of the strange gods that we have drifted from the truth to worship: stone idols, golden calves, mythological gods of the sun, of the moon, of the sea, of lightning, etc., temple statues, human sacrifice gods, birthplaces, mountains, kings, dictators, precious gems, gold, money, professional careers, intoxicants, drugs, possessions. A stone, the moon, a place, a dictator, a million dollars, a TV, is not God: created by God – yes, but not God.

I'm sure you can add to the list things that have taken the place of the true God in one's life. Even education, work, and computers, can become a focus of devotion and worship. It is not wrong to work hard, to pursue a career, or to obtain the best education that you can, as long as it does not become a priority to the exclusion of God or an obstacle to doing the will of God. In fact wealth, work, education, and devotion, all become assets when God's will is done.

"Hallowed be Thy name" supports why we were created. We are the only creatures on earth who can say hallowed be the name of God and who can understand the concepts inherent in the word hallowed. When we say "hallowed be Thy name," we are acknowledging our true God. We also speak for all life forms; we are nature's and creation's ability to say thanks for existence.

In summary, the words "hallowed be Thy name," reveal a one God: a God of truth, a God of good. They tell us how to acknowledge this God and they set the foundation for knowing truth.

Chapter 5

Thy Kingdom Come, Thy Will Be Done On Earth As It Is In Heaven

The phrase "Thy kingdom come" informs us that there is a place, or condition, or state of existence associated with God that can come about. The dictionary definition of the word kingdom that approaches the closest to a description of the kingdom of God is: a realm, community, or sphere in which one or something is dominant.[2] In the Prayer, "Thy kingdom come" is equivalent to "Thy will be done" – the phrase that follows it and ultimately defines it. As we proceed we shall see how this occurs and what constitutes this kingdom offered to us in the Lord's Prayer.

The section prayer, "Thy kingdom come, Thy will be done on earth as it is in heaven," can be interpreted in three different but related ways: as a statement, as a wish, and as a condition. Taken literally as a statement it says the kingdom of God will come and the will of God will be done on earth. This concise message means just what it says, no more or no less. It does not say how the kingdom will come or how the will of God be done but that they will occur. It implies that God will do it.

A second interpretation is seen as a request and a wish that the kingdom of God will come to us and that the will of God be done for us here on earth as it is in heaven. It is a prayer of hope from the people on earth to the God in heaven: a hope that God will bring the kingdom to us and that we will be granted entry into it. It implies faith and a trust in God to carry this out. It does not say how God will do it but expresses a belief that it can happen.

The third interpretation seen as a condition can be understood by placing the word if between the words come and Thy so that the prayer reads – Thy kingdom come if Thy will be done on earth as it is in heaven. This gives us another perspective showing us how the kingdom of God can come to earth: if God's will is done by the people on earth. We now have a formula for bringing the kingdom of truth, good, and as we will discover, love among us. The kingdom of God will come on earth as it is in heaven if we do the will of God on earth. It informs that we can have this kingdom on earth. It implies that the means to achieving this is up to us, individually and collectively.

These interpretations are not exclusive of one another and are not given to select one or the other. As we reflect on them we see, although providing different perspectives, they are interrelated and augment each other.

For the kingdom of truth, love, and good to come among us we need to know the will of God and how to do it; but, first we have to be clear as to what is implied in the word will. Will is defined as: that which is desired, especially a request, choice, or determination of the one having authority.[3] The will of God in the Lord's Prayer is a determination and a direction meant for us.

The will of God has been considered as anything that happens on earth and indirectly that is true. However, this is not the will expressed in the Lord's Prayer. Natural events, such as hurricanes, earthquakes, floods, are the result of fixed forces already in place for the creation and integrity of the planet earth.

Earthquakes occur when continental plates shift, collide, or separate, which they have been doing for billions of years: necessary to form our present landmasses, rivers, mountains, ranges, beaches, and ocean basins for our use now. Rain ends droughts and fills reservoirs. If there is excessive rain or snow, rivers have to swell to discharge the water. The continents have major rivers in place to drain them and for the commerce, travel, and recreational use of humanity.

We have been given the ability and the resources to take charge, through our will, to deal with the natural forces: to develop warning systems, build levees, reinforce our homes, avoid dwelling on flood plains, or building on barrier beaches, edges of cliffs, or crustal faults, to evacuate when necessary, and to provide relief and shelter when needed. With advances in discovery and cooperation we will be able to know about, predict, and utilize better the forces of nature. Within the realm of possibility are improved sophisticated warning systems, devised methods of preventing or altering catastrophic natural events, and harnessing for our use the electricity that arcs from the sky (lighting).

The will of God as referred to in the Lord's Prayer is directed to the will of human beings for their benefit – our benefit. How we should live in accordance with it has been revealed in several ways. God's will was precisely given in the Ten Commandments. They hold true today as they did over three thousand years ago.

To begin to understand the will of God we first need to review those God given commandments. They are as follows:

1. I am the Lord your God, you shall have no other gods before Me.

2. You shall not take the name of the Lord your God in vain.

3. Keep holy the Sabbath day. Six days you may work. Do no work, rest and give thanks on the seventh.

4. Honor your father and your mother.

5. You shall not murder.

6. You shall not commit adultery.

7. You shall not steal.

8. You shall not bear false witness against your neighbor.

9. You shall not covet your neighbor's house or belongings.

10. You shall not covet your neighbor's wife.

Some definitions and discussion regarding the commandments are as follows:

Other gods that can be placed and worshiped before the true God have been mentioned in Chapter 4. To the list we can add materialism and consumerism. To be devoted to material goods and objects to the exclusion of God is to make things false gods. To be excessive in our possessions can be an indication of devotion to things.

There is nothing wrong with having the best possessions that you can afford as long as you keep the perspective that they originate from God and are a gift to us from God. To be overly focused on the human body or on animals without acknowledgment of their creator can lead to misguided worship.

In vain by definition means: lacking in substance or worth, being unduly proud of one's appearance, not yielding the desired outcome, being irreverent.[4] We know that using the Lord's name in anger, in folly, as a joke or as a curse is irreverent. In vain also means to use the Lord's name falsely, without having true belief or substance, such as using it to impress others or just to gain attention and prestige.

Keeping holy the Sabbath, which for many is on Saturday or Sunday, can be any seventh day if you have to work weekends. The Sabbath day should be a day of rest and giving thanks to God; not losing focus by working unless it is a necessity. It should begin with acknowledging God and be spent in thankful recreation with either ourselves, our family, or with friends.

To honor father and mother includes forgiving them and caring for them if necessary. Murder is the killing of the innocent or any person who is not a threat to injuring or taking another's life. Adultery is having voluntary sex acts, including sexual intercourse, with an already married person. Covet means to enviously desire that which belongs to another person. It can lead to thinking of ways to obtain your neighbor's wife or husband or belongings. It can lead to degrading what we already have.

The Ten Commandments are definite, clearly understood, and possible to keep. As you review and reflect on them can you see ways they have been of benefit to us throughout the ages?

The will of God has also been shown to us through the life and teachings of Jesus Christ. If Jesus who gave us the Lord's Prayer said of God, "Thy will be done," then it follows that he would give us guidelines on how to do this will and he has. Jesus taught and lived the following:

Be merciful.

Be a peacemaker.

Do not insult others.

Do not be angry with each other.

Reconcile disputes with each other before going to court.

Do not judge others.

Do not be critical of others.

Look at your own faults first.

Do to others as you would have them do to you.

Love God with all your heart and mind and love your neighbor as yourself.

Love your enemies.

Pray for those who mistreat you.

Serve others.

Feed the hungry.

Clothe the naked.

Welcome the stranger.

Visit the sick, the dying, the prisoner.

Give to everyone who begs from you.

Do not give false oaths.

Say yes when you mean yes and no when you mean no.

Render to civil authority its due and to God, God's due.

Do not believe false prophets.

Teach others the Commandments.

Do not speak evil of you father and mother.

Forgive your children.

Do not divorce except on grounds of immorality (marital infidelity).

Do not despise little ones (children).

Be humble like a child.

Teach your children what is good. Do not lead them to evil.

Do not put God to the test.

Do not worry about tomorrow.

Do not be afraid.

Do the will of God.

Whomever does the will of God is brother, sister, and mother.

Trust God.

Like the Ten Commandments these guidelines are clearly stated; most are understandable and require no further elaboration in words. They are meant to be carried out in actions. Do not put God to the test means do not put your life at risk or in danger and challenge God to save you. We have the ability to judge what is right for our well-being and to preserve our life. God's laws in nature exist for a purpose. Jumping off a cliff and expecting God to float you back safely won't work. The law of gravity is already set in place. Staying behind and saying God will save you from a hurricane, when all advisories have been issued to evacuate, is putting God to the test.

The guidelines give us more insight into how to do the will of God and are able to be followed in our daily lives; in review, they define the good in human nature.

We can now address the question: what constitutes the kingdom of God? The guideline, whomever does the will of God is brother, sister, and mother, is the clue. The guideline implies that this kingdom, equivalent to the will of God, can come on earth through us, the subjects who are able to do God's will. Doing the desire of the One having authority is the step that leads to its manifestation and its connection. The kingdom of the Lord's Prayer then becomes the result of the assembly of those people who do or have done the will of the true God during their lifetime: the living who are doing God's will now and the dead whose lives' record is a testimony to having done God's will in the past. They have shown us the way to the kingdom.

At this point, now knowing the will of the true God, consider what the human condition would be like if all humanity did this will on earth. Can you see the possibility of a kingdom of truth, love and good coming upon and within us and our children: maybe not a possibility but a certainty.

God's will is also shown through three momentums that define a plan and purpose for existence. They are life, reproduction, and discovery. Termed momentums because they are entities that move forward in time and development towards a goal. They are clearly delineated. Being intrinsic conditions, forces within themselves that reflect the Creator's intentions, they are included under the will of God. Although separate by definition, they are connected in function. They move towards a common outcome.

The first momentum is life. Life is observed everywhere: in trees, flowers, grass, birds, bees and beetles, in fish, frogs, lizards, dogs, cats and raccoons, in deer, seals and elephants, in a man, a woman, a child. Our planet abounds with life: in the mountains, in the valleys, in the desert, in the forest, in the oceans, on the prairie, along the shoreline, in the villages and cities, on a busy highway, under the ground, over the ground, in the snow, in the air, on the land and in the waters. Earth has been aptly named planet life.

The momentum of life is growth developing to maturity: egg to adult, tadpole to bullfrog, baby to parent. Survival of the organism is the intrinsic condition; its purpose is to stay alive so that development and reproduction can take place. Whether it be bacteria, algae, a shrub, an earthworm, a salmon, a bluebird, a polar bear, or a human being, all will seek and grow in an environment that sustains its life and all life will reproduce if given the opportunity.

Volumes have been and will be written about life. However, the best way to know life is to meet it, observe it, reflect on it, participate in it, and to give thanks to God for it; since all life forms in any location and from any direction lead back to creation (to bring into being).

The second momentum is reproduction. As noted, the fact that all life aims towards reproduction shows the importance of this momentum. But, why is reproduction so important? It is through the dynamics of reproduction that the survival of the species is maintained. The intrinsic condition in life is survival of the organism; the intrinsic condition in reproduction is survival of the basic populations of organisms or species. The purpose of reproduction is to ensure and keep life forms in existence on our planet. This it does by transmitting the genetic code that programs the characteristics, growth, and development of the next generation; including the next generation's ability to reproduce – and so, the cycle of life goes on. Reproduction also provides a species with genetic reserve in case it has to adapt to changes in the environment that would affect it.

Any good biology book will describe the many and varied reproductive techniques: from simple splitting or binary fission, to the depositing of millions of eggs, to battles between the healthiest males for the right to impregnate the herd of females, to elaborate mating rituals including those of the human species. All are designed to insure that the species will survive – will continue existence.

Historically we have looked for the Creator in the big scene: in the sky, the mountains, the sun, the universe; however, it is in the DNA, RNA, chromosomes, the genetic code, that the forms and energy of life are determined. The Creator is also reflected in the minute but vital, little scene.

The third momentum is discovery. The continents, fire, water power, mathematics, tools, cement, vehicles, planes, boats, electricity, light bulbs, television, computers, the atom, medicines, skills, talents, creativity are a few examples and results of discovery. The momentum in discovery is the making known of the unknown, which then makes possible more discovery. The urge to know, explore, develop, invent, and create is the intrinsic condition.

The purpose of discovery is to safeguard the survival of the species, especially the human species, and to enhance the quality of life for all humanity. This is important not only for the comfort and efficiency of the human species, but also because we have been given authority over and the ability to manage and care for all other species. The human being stands between the Creator and all other forms of life. For example, the discovery of a heating system for homes during a northern winter ensures survival for families during those cold nights when the temperature is in the teens. They in turn bring in the plants that would die from the cold and shelter and feed the farm animals that would starve otherwise. To understand life forms, their needs, and uses, is a facet of discovery.

Discovery of one's skills, talents, and creativity leads to success for the individual and is a benefit to humanity. Discoveries of the father and mother are passed on from generation to generation. My father was an outdoorsman and fisherman. As a result, my children enjoy camping, the beach, bluefish, clams, and striped bass and my grandchildren love the life of the tidal pools.

Discovery appears to have a time for its occurrence and progression. Our forefathers walked a trail, then rode a horse, then had the comfort of a horse drawn carriage, then came the model T Ford, which led to a continually improved series of automobiles leading up to the current hybrid, low-gas-mileage vehicles of today; or, follow the progression from paddles to sails to steamboats to the latest high speed catamaran that almost flies across the water. All that we see newly constructed, our cities, highways and bridges, is the result of a progression of discovery. Whoever discovered the hammer did humanity a big favor.

Life, reproduction, and discovery define existence on earth; but more than that their intrinsic conditions, momentums, and goal directed purpose reveal an intelligence: an intelligence that designs, creates, and shows a plan. In this plan we are given an awareness and opportunity to participate: to participate by respecting and cherishing all life, by holding reproduction in the high level of dignity and awe it justly deserves, and by utilizing, appreciating, and enjoying discovery in ourselves and in others. The words respect, cherish, dignity, awe, appreciate, and enjoy are not used lightly or just for description. Any plan that creates, maintains, and improves our life is of utmost value and should be recognized as such. To discover the Intelligent Designer of the momentums is the ultimate discovery.

The Ten Commandments, the guidelines of Jesus, and the three intrinsic momentums (life, reproduction, discovery) offer to us the best instruction, direction, and hope for the well being of humanity. Their message in summed up in this short phrase: "Thy will be done."

Chapter 6

Give Us This Day Our Daily Bread

"Give us this day our daily bread," although sounding like a request, is first and foremost a prayer of awareness and acknowledgement. It conveys the awareness that God is the provider of our daily bread. When we say it, to whom do we look to – to give us our food, air, sunlight, and water? The prayer also affirms the image of God as the all good Father providing for His family. Yes, it is also a request prayer asking God to give us that which sustains us. It says give us our bread not the singular give me my bread indicating once again that we see ourselves as a human family, a community connected to each other under a providing God.

What is our daily bread? As symbolically stated it begins with bread or food. All foods: grain, nuts, fruit, vegetables, fish, fowl, meat, derivatives like eggs, cheese, soup, desserts and all liquids like water, juice, milk, coffee, tea, wine, beer, are given to us by God. Given to us that we may stay alive, stay healthy, and grow. Given to us that we may enjoy their fine tastes. Given to us with the potential to improve their quality and quantity. Given to us to provide income. Given to us to share with others. Given to us so that we can do the will of God by feeding the poor and hungry. Given to us to fulfill the momentums: life, reproduction, and discovery. Given to us so that we can appreciate the Provider and give thanks.

Our daily bread includes our basic life support: food, water, air, and the sun, without which we would lose our existence. It includes our natural resources such as ores, metals, plants, forests, oil, gas, electricity, and their derivatives, for example: homes, vehicles, appliances, clothing, and all materials that we use to improve our quality of life. Our daily bread is the herbs, vitamins, medications, and technology that we use to fight illness and disease. Our daily bread is the carbohydrate that nourishes our brain. It is all that stimulates our senses: sight, sound, touch, taste, and smell – our food for thought and creativity. Our daily bread includes the Word of God.

Orchids are a good example of being provided food for our senses and thought. They have recently evolved so that their presence would coincide with the age of humans. Orchid flowers are exquisitely beautiful to our eye; they protrude on a long stalk to catch our eye and grow at levels for optimal viewing. Orchids bloom for a long period and require minimal care, many getting nutrients through the air and having roots that require no soil. Orchids are designed not only to be enjoyed by humans but also to utilize humans as a means of propagation. By their ability to captivate our senses orchids use us as pollinators in order to reproduce and develop new varieties. Early prehistoric plants like ferns and cycads did not have flowers. There were no humans to attract and appreciate colorful blooms. Their purpose was to form coal. Flowers are a gift from God to be enjoyed by humans this day and orchids are a perfectly developed example.

Give us our daily bread also implies that we give thanks daily for what is given. Isn't it customary to say thanks to another when we receive an item, a gift, or an essential? Should it be different with God?

The plural, our bread, implies a collective ownership. True, farmers and manufacturers develop the products and are paid for their efforts. Distributors and retailers distribute and sell the products and are paid for their services. But in the Prayer is added the message that all God has provided for us is to be shared with all people everywhere. The collective ownership does not mean we have the right to trespass and take possession of what belongs to another. Do not covet. Do not steal. However, it does mean that the owner has the right to provide and share the bounty for the welfare of others. For us to share our belongings is to give us our daily bread.

The phrase "give us <u>this</u> day" puts the focus in the present, the here and now. Not yesterday which is past, not tomorrow which is future; but this day, now, which is reality and where the life experience currently exists. Using the words "this day," binds us to truth and truth is what really is. By emphasizing this day God wants us to be in the truth: to have our awareness in the present, not dwelling in the past or fantasizing about the future. God wants us to be alive in the now and to give thanks for the now. This day covers every day of our life in that if done "this day," yesterday and tomorrow are taken care of.

Thinking about the phrase "this day our daily bread," with its various levels of meaning, we begin to understand that the resources we have are in place to provide and be utilized for our existence in this day. Fossil fuels: coal, crude oil, and natural gas were processed and formed millions of years ago from then living sources now extinct. These energy fuels were stored through the centuries in underground reservoirs for our use this day: to heat our homes, run our vehicles, aircraft, ships, and to fuel our power plants. Electricity, like crude oil, was always available but waiting until discovered by the human mind at the right time with technology capable of utilizing its power: a power that lights our world and runs our machines and appliances. Dinosaurs and prehistoric animals could not discover electricity. They did not need it. Modern humans need it. All natural resources have a design, a purpose, and a time for their use, which is this day.

So the prayer, "Give us this day our daily bread," conveys an awareness of God as our provider, is a request to be provided for, and gives us the instruction to share what is provided with all others this day.

Chapter 7

Forgive Us Our Trespasses As We Forgive Those Who Trespass Against Us

This section prayer confronts a reality: the reality that we are capable of offending others, that others are capable of offending us, that we have weaknesses and failings, that we are not perfect, that we can and do take actions harmful to others and to ourselves, that we make mistakes. At the same time the prayer gives us a means for dealing with these imperfect aspects of human nature – forgiveness.

As a stated request, the prayer informs us that forgiveness is possible: possible for God, possible for us. I cannot presume to interpret God's forgiveness except to say, since it is alluded to in the Prayer, it can be given and obtained. "As we forgive," tells us that we also possess the ability to forgive.

We do not have to hold that grudge, do not have to wish harm or evil upon another, do not have to hurt, injure, or murder someone, do not have to retaliate against those who have trespassed against us. If forgiveness were not possible many in the world would continue to exist in a hostile, unhappy condition and many in the world still do.

What does trespass mean? According to the dictionary, trespass means: an unlawful act committed on the person, property, or rights of another.[5] In the Lord's Prayer trespass means to violate God's will in a way that affects another person. Some examples are: lying about another, cheating someone, stealing another's property, tempting someone, committing adultery, preventing others from doing the will of God, teaching others evil. Adultery, which violates God's will, not only affects the participants but also their spouses. I'm sure you can think of more examples of when you have been trespassed against and when you have trespassed against another.

Who is apt to trespass against us? Family members, such as: a husband who cheats on his wife and neglects his children, parents who teach their children hate, an adult who insults his or her parent, siblings who hold grudges over inheritance issues, neighbors who dispute with us, business people who cheat us. The violators range from close family and friends to strangers who rob, rape, or try to injure us, or may have killed a family member or friend. Yes, "as we forgive those who trespass against us" includes all, even those who commit the most violent crimes. Hard to accept but try to understand that we are forgiving the person, those who trespass, not the act of trespassing that violates. Judgment and justice regarding the act can take place on earth, such as mutual solving of disputes or through the courts. If not rendered on earth, judgment will be in the hands of God.

Parents have a special role in helping their children learn not to trespass against others. Children identify with their parents and want to act as they act. Some of the insidious violations that get passed on from generation to generation include: parents who physically or emotionally abuse their children, parents who teach their children prejudice by their own prejudice and resentment of others, parents who set an example of hating and injuring themselves, and parents who worship false gods and do not allow their children to be introduced to the true God.

At this point we should define what forgiveness is. According to the dictionary, to forgive means: to pardon or absolve, to stop being angry about or resentful against, to relieve from payment of.[6] To stop being angry about or resentful against comes closest to its intention in the Lord's Prayer at this time.

The early Greek translation of the Lord's Prayer says, "forgive us our debts as we forgive our debtors." Debts and debtors may have had a different application at that time than they do today.

However, be it debts or trespasses, the teaching of this section prayer is about forgiveness; not just forgiveness as defined in the dictionary, but the Lord's Prayer forgiveness: a forgiveness that contains the element of love.

There are degrees of forgiveness. At its basic level forgiveness can be just lip service. We say we forgive but do not feel it in our hearts and do not really agree with it in our minds; however, that is okay, since saying it is starting and aiming in the right direction. The next level of forgiveness requires a total attitude change so that you no longer carry the burden of resentment or anger towards another. You wipe away the grudge, the hate, and the hurt out of your mind. You begin to heal. The highest level of forgiveness is to love those who have trespassed against you: to love your enemies, to pray for those who persecute or have harmed you. It does not mean that you have to like them or feel an emotion towards them. Love as applied in forgiveness is not sentimental or emotional. It is a willful act of wanting the good and doing the good for another human being. It is an intention. To pray for those who have violated you is an act of love. Love wills good for another. Forgiveness then becomes a way that love is shown and shared: our love and God's love – the forgiveness of the Lord's Prayer.

We also need to forgive ourselves for trespassing against ourselves. "Forgive those who trespass against us" includes us. In fact we are probably the worst offenders: by being regretful, hating ourselves, bringing unhappiness upon ourselves, not taking care of our minds and bodies, injuring ourselves, and destroying ourselves by unhealthy habits or suicide. The same degrees of forgiveness hold true for us as they do in forgiving others. In fact, until we forgive ourselves it can be difficult to forgive others since we often look at others through the eyes of how we feel about ourselves. We should aim for wanting and doing the good for ourselves, in others words loving ourselves.

Forgiveness can vary in degrees and resolve. It can come and it can go. The deeper the hurt the harder to forgive and once forgiven the anger and resentment can re-occur. Then how often should we forgive? The answer is as often as necessary. In the Lord's Prayer there is no limit given on forgiveness. There is however a condition given and directed to us through the use of the word – <u>as</u>. "Forgive us <u>as</u> we forgive" clearly states that we have to do the forgiving and then we will be forgiven to the degree that we forgive. Forgiving now becomes a responsibility dependent upon us, which means all of us, all of us to do the forgiving. We are forgiven as we forgive tells us how God's forgiveness can be attained. Instead of a detailed, wordy instruction on how to receive this forgiveness, the Lord's Prayer tells us through one small simple word – <u>as</u>: concise, direct, amazing.

In this section we have defined and looked at some examples of trespass and forgiveness. In further chapters we will look at ways of dealing with trespass violations and ways of enacting forgiveness.

Chapter 8

Lead Us Not Into Temptation But Deliver Us From Evil

Would God lead us into temptation? I think not, because God is all good. Would God guide us away from temptation and evil? I think yes, because God is for the good for humankind. Love wills the good for the other and the true God is a God of love.

To begin to understand this section prayer view it as a request of children to a wise caring parent. A request to be led in the right direction and to be protected from harm. In reply, what do good parents do for the safety of their children? They set limits and guidelines to help them avoid trouble and danger. From our discussion in

Chapter 5 we know that the will of God is composed of limits and guidelines given to us for the well being of humanity; it then follows, that the will of the true God is what can deliver us from temptation and evil.

Temptation is anything that would lead us to not want to do the will of God. Some examples are: being given too much change at a store, knowing it and not wanting to be truthful by returning it, thinking of all the reasons you should not give any money to the poor, looking at your neighbor's wife too long, spending too much time with her especially when her husband is not home. Everyone everywhere is tempted and often when least expected. As you can see from the above examples, although there are external things, events, or people involved, temptation develops within us. We lead ourselves into temptation.

The answer to the prayer, "Lead us not into temptation," comes in two steps. The first step is discernment: meaning to detect and recognize something mentally, to be aware: the something in this case being temptation. The discernment step is to bring the risk of temptation into focus. The second step is the act of leading away from the something, event, or people that can lead us to not want to do the will of the true God. To take this step is to gain mastery over the temptation: to be in control. God wants us to be in control of our actions, which is one reason why we have minds and are able to discern. So, "Lead us not into temptation," is a prayer for discernment and the ability to take right action.

This prayer for discernment also includes, lead us not to be foolhardy and to use good judgment in all situations: in making major decisions, in how to use our money and resources, in how we develop our self-expression, and in how we use our time. We are given just so much time in our life span on earth. May we discern how best to use this time for our own optimal development and for the well being of others: our immediate family, and the human family.

Evil is the willful rejection of the true God in a way that is manifest by worshiping false gods and doing the opposite of God's will. Evil is the antithesis of God. If God is of truth, evil is deceit, lying, giving false witness. If God is of love and love your neighbor, evil is hate and harm your neighbor. If God is all good, evil is the rejection of all that is good which can lead to an effort to destroy the good.

An example of evil in its collective form became apparent in Nazi Germany raising its arm in worship to a delusional dictator, a false god, then destroying its neighbors and finally itself. Evil is destructive. Throughout history humans constructing and worshiping a false god and killing the innocent in the name of their false god have demonstrated the ultimate expression of evil. In its more subtle form evil exists when we willfully reject the true God's presence in our lives.

" Deliver us from evil" is a request and a prayer of hope: to save us from a potentially wretched existence, to protect us from destroying some or all of the human race. The design of the true God, as previously revealed, is for us to continue and care for the human race.

The use of the plural <u>us</u> has two significant applications in this section. First, leading us and delivering us applies to all of us, all people everywhere on earth. Remember in the beginning, the words, "Our Father," revealed that we are all connected. Second, even though we request God to do it, <u>us</u> infers that we have to share in the leading of us away from temptation and the delivering of us from evil. We also have a responsibility for the human condition.

"Deliver us from evil" implies distancing ourselves from evil. To deliver from is: to remove from, to get away from, to not linger with and gaze upon; lest we be tempted, led into, or subject to it.

So how do we meet this responsibility and lead each other away from temptation and evil? By understanding and doing God's will ourselves throughout each day, wherever we are, and in all situations: we then add to the collective good on earth. We also add to the good by our example to others. Good begets good; evil begets evil. If an opportunity presents, try to teach others about God and God's will for us on earth. The Prayer tells us not only to love our neighbor but also to work with our neighbor towards the common good.

It is of special value to teach children, whose minds are curious and receptive, about God and how to do God's will. Little children learn by the kindly spoken word and by observing the example of others especially their parents. Even though children have an innate tendency towards good they can be receptive to knowing and doing evil. It is up to us to not lead children into temptation and evil.

In summary, "Lead us not into temptation but deliver us from evil" is a request and a responsibility.

Chapter 9

The Prayer And Its Message

The Lord's Prayer informs us that there is a God. It describes this God and gives us insight into the nature of this God. These revelations are expressed through the four section prayers that together present a major theme disclosing a primary message from God to us.

Interestingly the word god is not mentioned in the Prayer; yet, the whole Prayer is a definition of a God. Who is this God that the Lord's Prayer defines and offers us? It is a God termed "Our Father," who exists in heaven, has a kingdom, has a will, can provide us all that we need, is forgiving, and can protect us from evil. This is the God of the Lord's Prayer.

Identifying God in one word, Father, gives us a concept that we can understand, but it implies more. Fathers are real. We have all had one. Their existence is true. The word, Father, besides showing us a God who is like a good father, designates a God who is true. The adjective true, with a small t, does not mean an only god or an exclusive god. It simply means what true means – not false. Identifying God as a true God, not a false god, is important since upon this true God we put our belief, our hope, and our trust.

The Prayer continues to reveal more aspects of this true God through our understanding of the section prayers. The prayer, "Our Father who art in heaven, hallowed be Thy name," acknowledges and respects God as a God of truth. The prayer, "Forgive us our trespasses as we forgive those who trespass against us", shows us a God who forgives, a God of love. The prayer, "Give us this day our daily bread and lead us not into temptation but deliver us from evil", tells us of a God who wills good for humanity, a God that is all good. These section prayers reveal to us a God of truth, love, and all good.

Whereas father is a true concept: truth, love, and good are forces. Forces that are also true, that exist, that are real. Forces that we can see, experience, and act upon; forces that have power. And what is the power of truth, love, and good? Power to motivate. Power to initiate. Power to educate. Power to create. Power to appreciate. Power to love. Power to forgive. Power to heal. Power to trust. Power to spread. Power to bring peace. When we say God the Power, think of what is implied.

The God, whose essence has now been revealed to us as the power of truth, love, and good, will from now on be referred to as True God: True with a capital T. This is done for lack of a more precise descriptive name. Now a name is just a name; it's what the name stands for that matters. True God stands for the power of truth, love, and all good.

" Hallowed be Thy name," using the name True God, infers that truth, love, and good are hallowed: in other words, brought to a high level of respect in which we should hold them. They reflect the nature of God and when we show truth, love, and do good we embody God's essence and power – we become the image of God.

All the section prayers that build the Lord's Prayer present a theme within the Prayer that formulates its main message: a message meant for and given to us by the True God. Central to this theme is forgiveness around which the Prayer revolves and is the foundation for the message. The message that comes through the Lord's Prayer is: love God and love your neighbor as yourself. Now, how do we understand this and how is the message derived?

A summation of the message is expressed when we say "Our Father who art in heaven, hallowed be Thy name, forgive us our trespasses as we forgive those who trespass against us." In other words: love and respect God, forgive and love your neighbor and yourself. The keystone words, upon which the message is constructed and from which the message is interpreted, are hallowed and forgive. Two words from which comes an instruction and a prayer given to help humanity.

In the message love is used twice and has two relevant meanings. To love God means to believe in the God of the Lord's Prayer, to focus your mind, heart, and trust upon the essence of this God and to pursue truth, love, and good throughout your life. In other terms, it translates into being aware of the True God each day and doing God's will, which as we shall see is living the Lord's Prayer.

The second use of love says love your neighbor as yourself. In this context love means to will good and do good to others as yourself. As means likewise, likewise means also; which translates into love others and also yourself: a love that goes both ways, willing and doing good to others and to yourself. Although the two loves as defined in the message have different directions, one towards God, one towards others and ourselves, they are similar in that when fulfilled they become acts of love.

The most significant word in the Lord's Prayer is <u>us</u>. Give us, forgive us, lead us, deliver us: all connect us to God and make us the recipients of God's word. The Prayer's insights, guidelines, and message have been given to us. Using the word us also connects us to each other, establishing a family network through which all are related in God. Implicit in the use of the word us is – help each other. Us conveys that we can receive and can give truth, love, and good to ourselves and to others, and when we do this we fulfill the divine message, put the words of the Prayer into action, and reflect the True God.

The first half of the Prayer tells us not only to love God but also shows us how to love God: by acknowledging God as our Father, by holding hallow God's name, and by doing the will of God. That's it. The second half of the Prayer tells us not only to love our neighbor and ourselves but also shows us how to love our neighbor and ourselves: by sharing our daily bread, by forgiving, and by not leading into temptation and evil. That's it.

The Lord's Prayer is a wonderful paradox in that at the same time we say it, asking God to help us, the Prayer is talking to us telling us what we can do to receive God's help and to help each other.

If you do not reflect or meditate on anything else in the Prayer think on one or more of just three words: hallowed, forgive, and us. God most holy, God of forgiveness, God who comes to us.

The Prayer ends with a mission: a mission to carry out for the well being and survival of humanity – "Deliver us from evil." This mission, given to us in the plural, clearly means that we participate in delivering ourselves, our children, and our neighbors from evil. We can begin with ourselves.

Chapter 10

Why Say The Lord's Prayer?

The Lord's Prayer tells us that there is a True God whose essence is the power of truth, love, and good. The Prayer informs us that this God is our creator and provider of all that we have. It says that this Provider is loving and caring by showing a love expressed in giving and forgiving; and that we can also share in this love by our own giving and forgiving. It tells us that if we do the will of this God, good will prevail in our lives. The Prayer also states that we can be protected from temptation and evil: forces that can destroy truth, love, and good on earth. Are we capable of believing this? I think yes. Are we capable of fulfilling these teachings through action? I think yes. By saying the Lord's Prayer we make it a reality and attest to its validity and relevance in our present life. Most important, when we say the Prayer we bring truth, love, and good into our presence.

We function better and accomplish more with truth than with lies: education, wisdom, justice are examples that give testimony to truth. We live better, feel better, and survive longer with love than with hate: peace, a hospital, a meal, are examples that give testimony to love. Common sense, history, and our own experience, show us that the human condition is better under good than under evil.

If the Lord's Prayer can lead us to experience truth, love, and good, is it not worth saying?

If saying the Prayer contributes to the force of good on earth and against the force of evil is it not worth the effort?

Try to visualize a humanity whose foundation is built on truth, love, and good. Saying and living the Lord's Prayer is laying that foundation.

In the following chapter we will look at how the Lord's Prayer can help us personally.

Chapter 11

How Does The Lord's Prayer Help Us?

Agood father is security for his family. Even though at times he may not be present, his wife and children have the ease of mind to function normally, knowing that he is providing for and looking out for their well being. Love and trust develops in that family. Believing in God as a good father and trusting as a child can give us a similar sense of security.

As a child looks up to his or her father for supportive strength, our seeing God as the One who has authority, power, and love can give us the courage to face whatever adversity comes our way. Picture the comfort and support that a sick child has, knowing his or her father is at the bed-side looking over them.

The plural, "Our Father", informs us that we are not alone with our individual problems. There is a powerful God who created us and knows all our needs. That God is not only looking over us but also has given us members of the human family who can help if we ask. The physician, the therapist, the grocer, the auto mechanic, the car-penter, a roofer, a volunteer, our neighbor are a few examples. It helps with our understanding and appreciation to see all good service works as an extension of the arm of God.

The needs and problems of humanity are uni-versal. There are others who have experienced and understand our situation. The way to receive help for what troubles us is to ask for it: to ask God the Father, and to ask another human. For help to be given it has to be received and we have to be of a mind to accept it. The outcome may not be as we would like it, but it may be as God would allow it. Our ways are often not God's ways. The Lord's Prayer guides us towards God's way.

"Who art in heaven," "Thy kingdom come," are two statements that give us hope for an existence after death. They set the foundation for trusting in God that there is a life hereafter. This belief is important to all who cherish life and especially sustaining to those who are close to dying and to the family members of deceased relatives. Saying the Lord's Prayer helps us to deal with death.

"Thy will be done" not only informs that there is a will of God for us but also that it can be done in our lives here on earth. To do the will of God fulfills the message of the Prayer and gives the human race a purpose for existing. The Lord's Prayer provides a guide to living. If the will of God be done on earth as it is in heaven our existence here would be one of love not hate, life not killing, truth not falsehood, shared abundance not deprivation. Being human as God wills it would be maximized. The Lord's Prayer brings out the best in humanity.

"Forgive us our trespasses as we forgive those who trespass against us," deserves special focus since this section prayer is the only way God's will is directly shown throughout the whole Prayer. The Prayer does not say give us as we give others, lead us as we lead others, deliver us as we deliver others, those are all implied; but, so there is no doubt as to its intention, it says "forgive us as we forgive others." The great message lies hidden in the Prayer. The will of God has to be understood from other teachings. Giving, leading, and delivering others have to be interpreted. But, the way to forgiveness is made perfectly clear. Forgiveness must be important and must be of value to us.

How does forgiving others help us? To truly forgive can free us from the burden of carrying the weight of grudge, hate, revenge, hurt feelings, depressed and angry moods. If we are still suffering over a past hurtful offense that no longer exists except in our mind, to keep dwelling on it keeps the event and associated stress alive in our body. To forgive helps to seal it back into the past where it belongs. This can reduce tension and improve our focusing in the present. It takes a load off our mind and our body. If there was no real violation and we are creating the trespass in our thinking, or if the violation was a minor non intentional act which we are magnifying out of proportion, then forgiving the imagined violator corrects a false belief and brings us back to reality. Forgiving another may not have any effect on that actual or imagined offender but it can have a positive healing effect on the forgiver.

We can make the other person who they are to us. If, in our mind, we construct them as bad, they become bad to us. If we construct them as good, they become good to us. If someone has a drug addiction problem are they bad? If they steal or beg to support their problem are they bad? Is the drug addiction bad? Is the stealing bad? Can that person with the bad habit change? Can they be loved? Can they love? To forgive puts the label we have placed on them aside and sees them for what they are, a troubled person with a serious problem needing help.

If your son or daughter leaves to follow and become victim to all the vices of the world and then returns to your home depressed, burned out, or broke, can you forgive them? Are they bad? Are they good? Are they who they are? Forgiving does not mean that you have to tolerate or ignore the problem. Forgiving is an act of the will directed towards the person or offender with the problem. When forgiveness leads to helping that person it becomes an act of love. The message in the Prayer is love your neighbor and an act of love may indeed have a good effect upon the recipient.

How often should we forgive and help another? I was told about an "alcoholic" who was picked up out of the gutter and brought to a hospital for care. As soon as he was discharged he would drink and wind up shaking or convulsing in the gutter again. After being retrieved out of the gutter twenty-five times he stopped drinking and never returned to that gutter.

Do not judge others can ease up or even dispel fear, social anxiety, anger, and false thinking. It contributes to a more realistic understanding and interaction with others, especially strangers. To have an initial fear or anxiety upon meeting the stranger is natural. It is an instinct we are born with and serves as a protective mechanism during childhood. Through growing up and meeting strangers who then become friends we learn that the best way to over-come stranger fear is to get to know them. This is important if we have been taught prejudice by our families, have preconceived negative attitudes towards those different from ourselves, or carry an inferiority attitude towards ourselves in comparison to others. Often by getting to know the stranger we find out that inside they are just like us though they may look, dress, and talk differently. Welcome the stranger is not only meant for the stranger's sense of acceptance – it is also meant for ours.

We can do to ourselves the same injustice by judging ourselves. We may hate ourselves or want to injure or even kill ourselves because of self-judgment. Should we deny ourselves the chance to make amends and try to improve our attitude and our life? To love your enemy includes the enemy within us: that enemy that demeans, berates, diminishes our self worth, judges us falsely, and may ultimately destroy us.

Judging ourselves falsely is often based on someone else's judgment of us. This can develop when parents label their child as bad, no-good, good for nothing. They may reinforce this belief by verbal or physical abusive acts towards their child. The child who is good, all children are good in God's plan, grows up with the voice of the judgmental parent in his or her mind telling them they are no-good and they believe it. As an adult the grown child continues to accept this false script. They may even try to live up to their parent's negative opinion of them by acting no-good. The teaching of the Lord's Prayer to not judge and to forgive and love others and ourselves helps us to combat the enemy within. Again the use of the plural us implies that we may need the help of others: loving family, friends, self-help groups, professional help. The enemy within can be deeply rooted.

Do not judge others is associated with forgiveness, therein lies its value. Suspending judgment is the pathway to forgiveness. Forgiveness is the way to love. Love is the message of the Prayer and that message is for our good. Judgment like for-giveness does not mean we are to accept or tol-erate offensive acts and disturbing behavior. Do not judge others means just that; do not judge the person. Use good judgment regarding the act or behavior. Involve family, proper authority, or professional help if necessary, even avoidance if required, and let God be the final judge.

Forgiving parents is implied in the command-ment "Honor your father and mother." We may not like the way our parents treated us. We may hate and resent the offensive acts they committed upon us when we were young. We may even blame ourselves for their actions even though at the time we were the child and they the adult. But, "forgive those who trespass against us" means all mem-bers of the human family, which includes our parents, living and dead. For those still suffering from past parental traumas, forgiving can break the chains that bind them to the past, helping them to move on and be better parents to their children. Many parents who abuse their children have been abused themselves as children and still carry the hurt and anger, which they take out on their own children. Forgiveness helps break the cycle.

Forgiveness, as presented in the Lord's Prayer, is for our good. It is for us. If our forgiving helps the other it is incidental. The other person may not even be aware that you have forgiven them and may not even care. Your forgiveness may have no effect on them whatsoever; but it can have an effect on you. Forgiveness, as given to us, is to help us deal with our anger and resentments. It is given to us to help free us from holding on to past hurts. It is given to us to improve our focus in present reality. It is given to us to help us have peace of mind. It is given to us to help us relate to our human family.

Having defined the True God as a God of truth, love, and all good, it would seem that those attributes would be main elements in God's forgiveness. We are forgiven "as we forgive" says that we also have a part in God's forgiveness and it could be a major part. Our record of forgiveness may be the determinate of how God forgives us. The

Lord's Prayer may be informing us and preparing us for that eventuality.

Leading ourselves not into temptation is so important for the quality of our life. Most mature adults know their temptations. We all are tempted in various ways and have had unhealthy habits and behaviors. We can pray to God to lead us from temptation and this is important in setting the goal. We then have to become part of the leading by taking an action and, if we are incapable of taking action, utilizing the help of others. Therein lies an answer to our prayer, for God has given us others to help us to avoid temptation.

For example: I recall the man who had an alcohol dependence problem that was wrecking his life. I met him while he was hospitalized in an alcohol rehabilitation program. On his first weekend pass he took a bus 100 miles to his home. Upon arriving he found his wife was not at home and a six-pack of beer had been left in the refrigerator. He was being led towards temptation. He immediately turned around, left the house, and took a bus back to the hospital. He took an action to lead himself not into temptation but he also needed the help of others for that very scenario, of being confronted with alcohol, was role-played at the hospital before he left, including the abrupt walking away and returning. That is what helped him. He did not do it alone. When we invoke God's help to lead us not into temptation we are calling upon a power that works through others and within ourselves.

Evil was defined in Chapter 8 as the willful rejection of the true God and worshiping of false gods. All the wars that have been fought throughout history, the wars that are fought now, and the wars yet to come, involve some element of combating the evil force. Yes, evil is a force, a destructive force that can captivate us and spread through us.

How does the Lord's Prayer help us to deal with evil? When said it brings truth, love, and good into our presence: a powerful shield against evil. When tempted or confronted by evil say the Lord's Prayer. Say it again and again and again if necessary. If someone you know is captured by evil say the Prayer for them with an intention to free them from its grip. Meet evil head on by living the Lord's Prayer, for every act in living it counters an evil act.

Although the Prayer can be a shield, sometimes we have to do more as the arrows of evil keep coming. If you are inclined towards evil make an effort to incline in the other direction. Attend church or synagogue, read the Bible, join a prayer group, keep physically active, keep occupied with good works, and seek professional help if needed. Keep the guard up daily and make it a life's goal.

The best preventative against evil for adults is living the Lord's Prayer. For children, it is their parents setting the good example, being involved with their children, and allowing their children into their lives.

Many people live their whole life or portions of their life in fear: fear of others, fear of the neighbor, fear of confrontation, fear of authority, fear of retaliation, fear of speaking out, fear of trying, fear of making a mistake, fear of failure, fear of success, fear of humiliation, fear of rejection, fear of eternal damnation, fear of the unknown, fear of being laughed at, fear of being yelled at, fear of being spanked. The list goes on. Much of the fear that we carry stems from an underlying fear of punishment or embarrassment: fears instilled in us from childhood experiences.

Now, fear is not necessarily negative. It is what it is. It can be motivating. It can be hindering. It can lead to wise decisions and appropriate action. It can cause avoidance and inhibition. It can keep us from getting into trouble. But fear becomes a negative in one's life when it prevents self-actualization, fulfillment, happiness, and joy in living. To those blocked by fear the Lord's Prayer offers a subtle message: do not be afraid, you have a Father in heaven whose kingdom is coming, who has given you guidelines in living, who provides for your needs, who forgives, who leads away from temptation and evil, who is powerful. Implicit in this subtle message is trust your Father.

Many fears are deeply rooted in our mind, especially the fear of punishment; other fears are appropriate to a threatening situation. Saying and living the Lord's Prayer may not lessen or alleviate fear; but it may. One thing that saying, living, and trusting in the Lord's Prayer will do however, is help us to face the fear, to deal with it, and act in spite of it. Many people have prayed before facing a fearful event, such as going on stage, or on a dangerous mission, or before an interview with authority, or when facing death. Saying the Lord's Prayer in the face of fear is an action aimed at coming to grips with it. Repeating the Lord's Prayer every time the unwanted fear arises is fighting back and may indeed wear the fear down and out.

Is there an unseen power in saying the Lord's Prayer? So far we have looked at the powers that can be defined, observed, or identified with. For example: when said the Prayer brings good into the present, it influences good acts, it consoles those who mourn, it gives strength to those who suffer, it helps deal with fear, it encourages for-giveness, it fosters unity, it increases faith. The Prayer has individual, personal power effects for those who say it, but if we say it for someone else or for a cause can it have an effect on that person or on that cause?

My response to that question is that much of what we see and are aware of now was at one time unseen: automobiles, jetliners, a moon rocket, television, computers, E-mail, satellites, atomic energy. Who would have seen all these two hundred years ago? At that time the speed of communication was as fast as a horse could go. Like our modern day E-mail, might a prayer, when said for another person, travel fast and direct and be instantly received by that person? Can praying for a cure effect a cure in someone else? Many will attest to being cured by acts of prayer from others. So I leave it to those affected or not affected to decide. The unseen power of the Prayer is something that you have to believe in and experience to make seen.

Chapter 12

Saying The Lord's Prayer

When Jesus gave humanity the Lord's Prayer he said, "When you pray go into your room, shut the door and pray in secret and God who sees in secret will reward you." Does that mean that the prayer should not be said in public? No, because Jesus never said not to say it publicly. He gave the instruction to pray privately for several reasons. In the context of the times he was telling his disciples not to pray like the hypocrites who prayed in public to demonstrate how holy they were. To pray in secret safeguards us from doing the same, from praying to impress others, from giving a false impression, from using the Prayer in an insincere or frivolous way.

Saying the Lord's prayer in secret diminishes distractions, allows us to pray at our own pace, and most important enhances our individual relationship with God who sees in secret.

Praying the Prayer in the secret of your room means not only in your home but also in the secret room of your mind, no matter where you are. In this busy day and age many spend little time at home except to eat or sleep and when there, they are tired, or demanded of, or have other responsibilities. Praying in secret in your mind can be anywhere: in the car waiting at a red light or while stuck in traffic, sitting in the airport or on a plane, riding the subway, in a restaurant awaiting a meal, in the crowded stadium before the event, walking in a garden, standing in a quiet museum. I am sure you can add more places where the Lord's Prayer can be said in the secret room of your mind. The Prayer takes me 45 seconds to say and I pray slowly.

When praying the Lord's Prayer aloud in public, either in a small group or larger gathering, it is still coming from within us but now has an added social aspect. Others are present. Others are saying it. Others are listening. It becomes a public prayer. Public prayer can be supportive and inspirational. It can be especially helpful to those with special needs or going through a difficult time. Praying out loud before a group can help develop self-confidence and sense of social acceptance. It can strengthen faith. Being united in prayer reminds us that we are all related through God. This will become apparent if you look around as you say the Prayer with others.

Saying the Lord's Prayer as a family or couple, either at home or in public, can provide the benefits of public prayer plus enhance family unity. It can help deal with family needs and teach the good example to children. Family prayer should be said in a spirit of love, forgiveness, and mutual respect. If the Prayer is discussed, any messages contributed by the family members should be listened to. A married couple praying together as they travel through life have a guiding aide to help them deal with what life gives them, its ups and downs.

Often when finishing the Lord's Prayer we say amen which seals the end of the Prayer; then quickly we move on to the next agenda. This is okay because it is the act of saying the prayer that matters. However, the Prayer was given to us not only to be said but also to be listened to: to listen for any thoughts, insights, and messages that come to us while praying it and when pausing after it is said.

A message if it comes will permeate your upper body, being heard and felt in the head, neck, and chest. It comes to and through your inner self. It will be brief and pertinent to your present life. Some messages I have received are: Be Patient, Enjoy The Day, Appreciate Your Wife, Enjoy Family Members (sons, daughters, grandchildren who are visiting), Do Not Be Afraid. Whenever I receive the message to be patient I know my patience will be tested sometime during that day and it always is. To receive a message from prayer we have to believe we can and we have to listen. To develop the skill of listening we have to listen for what the Prayer teaches, listen to our thoughts stimulated by it, and listen for any messages that come to us through it. All are of value for our well-being; all enhance the quality of our life.

The Lord's Prayer can be said with or without personal intentions. Having an intention adds your love to the Prayer for it wills good for the other. Some intentions include saying the Prayer: for someone who is sick or dying, for our parents, children or relatives, for our neighbors or neighborhood, for government leaders, for those in harms way, for the peace makers, for those suffering natural disasters, for the deceased and their families, for victims of evil acts, for those committing evil acts, for someone who needs a prayer. Intentions can include giving thanks to God for all that we have, for all that is beautiful, for all that is good; or specific thanks such as for the birth of a child, a successful operation, good health, the return of a member to the family.

Saying the Lord's Prayer with intention may or may not have an obvious effect on the recipient or the cause but it has a direct effect on the sayer. It provides a satisfying sense of doing something for another. It leads us to think of the good for someone or some event. It instills appreciation. It becomes an act of love for us and by us. When we say the Lord's Prayer without any intentions, it fulfills its own intentions as given in the section prayers. It brings truth, love, and good within us.

Sometimes we can concentrate on each word of the Prayer and pray with feeling and devotion. Other times the Prayer is said in an automatic, non thinking, non feeling way. We are not in the same frame of mind all the time. There may be distractions, issues that preoccupy us, wandering thoughts. We may be mentally tired, worn down, worried. Repeating the Prayer and trying to visualize each word in your mind might help. Sometimes closing your eyes while saying it will help. Sometimes nothing helps but that is all right. There is no need to judge its quality or intensity since the act of saying the Prayer is the important step.

The Lord's Prayer being composed of section prayers can also be prayed in sections as the thought, need, or desire arises, or for a pause in a busy routine. It is alright to honor God and profess a faith and trust in God by just saying "our Father who art in heaven hallowed be your name." It is alright to ask God for help by saying "our Father give us this day our daily bread," or "our Father lead us not into temptation," or "our Father forgive us or forgive me." These specific prayers are said briefly and directly to God. Praying a section prayer is not an abbreviation or substitute for saying the complete Prayer: a wonderful synthesis of prayers, themes, messages, and direction. When saying the Prayer, try to focus it inwards, into your inner self, as that is where our connection to God lies.

There is no reason to embellish the Lord's Prayer with a lot of words. It is not necessary. As given the Prayer says what it says perfectly. Each word fits and builds the whole. All other human well intentioned prayers are subsidiaries of it. It deserves appreciation and respect. It is the Word of the True God.

Chapter 13

Living The Lord's Prayer

Another wonderful paradox of the Lord's Prayer is that it was given to us to be said as a prayer and when prayed it is meant to be lived. To live the Lord's Prayer is to do the Lord's Prayer. To do the Lord's Prayer is to put the section prayers into action. How to do this?

As the Prayer begins by acknowledging God as our Father, we can begin each day with thanking God for the blessing of the day. It does not require many words to give thanks; it is the act and intention that counts. An example is, "I thank you God for this day" or any variation that you like. That's all that need be said. Following the act of thanks the Lord's Prayer should be said. The Prayer should be said a least once a day preferably in the morning but of course can be prayed more often as desired or needed.

Saying the Lord's Prayer at a time of natural beauty or inspiration such as a stunning sunset, a clear cold starry night, on a high vista, a mountain or bridge, or at the water's edge, makes the Prayer an act of thanks for the creation of the beautiful world around us. Saying it for the intention of others, those around us, those not present, strangers, or family, makes it an act of love. Saying it for those who have offended us makes it an act of forgiveness. Saying it for someone or others trapped in temptation or evil makes it an act of deliverance. Saying it for yourself makes it an act of strength.

When we pray we ask God to give us our daily bread, which includes all that sustains and stimulates our life. Since God does give us our daily bread it is appropriate that we give thanks. The best time to do this is when utilizing these gifts. For example, when drinking water or washing up, swimming or fishing, thank God for the water, thank God for the fish. Giving thanks can include: thanks for the air, thanks for the sunlight, thanks for the stars, thanks for vision to see the stars, thanks for the tree, thanks for the color green, thanks for vision to see the color green, thanks that my kidneys work, thanks for my medicine. I'm sure you can think of many more basic thanks. Keep them specific and for things that you need and appreciate. Set a goal to give God thanks at least once a day for something that keeps your mind and body alive. A simple thanks will do.

A special thanks should be given before each meal for the actual food provided to us. It can be said aloud or in silence. It can be said by one person or joined by many. It is especially important to say it aloud with children present. They will benefit from hearing it. Again a lot of words are not important; the act of giving thanks is. To say "We thank you God for our daily bread" or some version of that is enough said. If it is a holiday or if you have guests or extended family at the table, giving thanks for their presence to share the meal with can be added.

Dining at someone else's home, they may say thanks. If not and you feel it appropriate you could ask that thanks be given. If not appropriate say your silent thanks. In a restaurant, the setting will determine if thanks be said aloud or in silence. It is the act that counts.

Following the Ten Commandments and God's guidelines as given in Chapter 5 is important for putting the Lord's Prayer into action. They are the will of God and by living them – "Thy will be done." At this point it would be helpful to review Chapter 5 with an eye towards how the Commandments and guidelines can be put into action in our lives. It will help towards living the Prayer.

Giving to charities either time or money will help the poor, feed the hungry, clothe the naked, serve the sick, the aged, and children in need; and we can do that from the comfort of our home. Select charities that are reliable in doing the will of God. By connecting with them you are then doing the will of God also. As a guide ten percent of one's income is an advised amount, but any amount even the smallest will be helpful. It all adds up and the act counts.

Visit the sick, the grieving, and those in prison: not just your family, but friends and neighbors also. For some it is hard to go into a hospital or to a wake, if so send a get-well or sympathy card. If not a card, then say a Lord's Prayer with intention. Welcoming the stranger not only helps them to feel less strange and fearful, but also will help you by dispelling your fears and fantasies about those new people. During a time of disaster, such as a hurricane, tornado, earthquake, or flood, volunteer to help those in need: either through direct service, a public service agency, or by contributing money, food, or supplies. Live the Lord's Prayer.

Saying love your neighbor and yourself is a fine concept but how do we put that love into an act of expression? It is done by helping another. Helping another fulfills the directive given in the word us and gives purpose to the extensive diversity of talents, skills, and abilities that we have been given. Helping another in any manner, from pacifying a crying baby to building a house for someone, is living the Lord's Prayer. Our abilities have not developed within us for nothing.

Be a peacemaker. Where there is resentment, anger, and hurt feelings try to provide a solution, try to keep calm, rational, and forgiving. Do not feed into the anger or say and do things that intentionally escalate it. Say I am sorry if indicated; walk away to calm down if necessary. If you see children fighting or bullying each other, intervene and tell them it is not a good thing to do. Try to help by listening to their complaints and how they are feeling. Ask them to try to be friends. Tell them it is better to be friends than to hurt each other. The aggressive child or bully may be dealing with disturbing family issues usually involving their relationship or lack thereof with their dads. Sometimes they have a condition such as attention deficit hyperactivity disorder that may need professional help.

If there is a family member or neighbor that you are carrying anger towards or vice versa, contact them either in person, by phone, or by mail if necessary. Let them know what is bothering you and that you would like to resolve it. You are attempting to confront an issue and to make peace with yourself and with that person. It may help. If it does not, congratulate yourself for trying to be a peacemaker. The act of trying is of value. If your act does not bear immediate results it may do so later on. Be patient.

Being a peacemaker also means to make peace with yourself. Forgiving yourself and others is so important for living the Lord's Prayer. To berate yourself, call yourself names, despise and hate yourself, keeps the conflict within alive. It keeps you from improving your self worth, from finding your peace of mind, from progressing comfortably with your life. Yes, you should regret the selfish, hurtful acts that you have done to others, but if the act is over and you have resolved not to commit the offensive trespass again, you are on the way towards self-forgiveness. If possible contact the person you have hurt, tell them you are trying to change, that you are sorry for what you have said or done. This can be helpful in bringing estranged family members together again. By sincerely asking your family member to forgive you, you help forgive yourself and may be helping them to deal with a long held hurt and resentment. If your attempt is not received, you have tried to be a peacemaker. Congratulate yourself for making the effort.

We should not use forgiveness as an excuse to continue doing harmful acts to ourselves and others. Along with the words I forgive has to come an effort to change. Do whatever it takes. Saying the Lord's Prayer daily is a start.

Always try to solve the anger generating issue between you and the other person first before bringing in a third party, or calling law enforcement, or going to court. Do not let fear or anger build up inside and not deal with it. Neither is good for your health. Resort to others and the law if it becomes necessary. Most of our laws were established to keep the peace or protect neighbors and family members. Domestic violence laws are an example.

Do not lead others into temptation or towards evil. We should try to lead others to the God of truth, love, and good first by our example: by being truthful and honest in our interactions, by willing good for others, and by doing good acts. Whenever you can teach about God, try to. The seed of your good example and teaching may not be apparent now but may develop in someone later in life especially when needed.

It is important for parents to guide their children to an awareness of God. First, by the good example of avoiding evil. Children always identify with their parents, want to please them, and often turn out like them in various degrees. Do not set evil examples. If you do commit an offensive act and your family finds out, set a determination to change, quietly forgive yourself and then ask for their forgiveness. Resolve not to commit the evil act again. Children are very forgiving towards their parents but will be hurt by betrayal.

Teaching children about God can take several directions such as going to prayer groups, church, synagogue or temple, together with the father present. Making sure children have some type of religious education such as Sunday school, catechism, Bible study, and responding to their curiosity and questions about God can all be helpful depending upon how they are given and received. At the least they will provide an awareness of God. What can also be helpful is the family sitting together and discussing God in the form of scripture from the Bible. There are parents who are unable to, or are not comfortable with, attending public religious services but that does not mean they cannot introduce their children to God. A reading from the Old or New Testaments and then discussing it will do. A half hour or more if interest is present will be enough. Doing the family reading on the Lord's day will emphasize the significance of that day but any day is good.

Parents should allow their children opportunity to express their thoughts about the Bible readings and about God even if the thoughts are contrary. If discussion, explanation, and correction are necessary it should be done in a patient, loving manner. Parents should not be critical or domineering as the interaction between family members is as important a teacher as the words being discussed – maybe more important.

Good, caring interaction with children safeguards them from temptation and evil. An example of good interaction is when the parents, especially the fathers, attend their children's school programs, performances, or sports events. Just being present will benefit everyone. There is not room enough to list all the sons and daughters that excelled in sports because their fathers were present and supportive of them. But, they are just the tip of the iceberg. They are the ones that achieved public notice. Underneath are all the adult children who have developed good characters, lead good lives, help others, and raise their families because their fathers, or a father figure, or trust in a higher father power, was present in their lives. Our jails and prisons are full of other adult children who are there because they did not have good, caring family interaction. Their fathers let them down. We have not even scratched the surface in our understanding of the tremendous power of the father.

Last but not least trust the True God. We are not living the Lord's Prayer by ourselves. We do our part; we try and then make an act of trust by simply saying "Lord I trust in you, please be with me." Say it even if you are doubtful and do not feel the trust. Ask that trust and the self-confidence that accompanies it will develop. Trust builds confidence. God has said, "Knock and it shall be open to you, seek and you shall find." Trust will help us to do the knocking and the seeking and the finding.

Trusting in God does not exempt us from the human condition: tragedy can happen, illness may occur, growing old and death will surely come. However, trusting in God and living the Lord's Prayer will help us to confront and deal with those unwelcome events. It will put them in proper perspective.

The following outline of the twelve discussed ways of living the Lord's Prayer is shown as a summary review for the sake of clarity. As you review the list you may see more personal choices to add to it.

Live the Lord's Prayer by:

- Giving thanks to God for this day.
- Saying the Lord's Prayer at least once a day.
- Giving thanks daily for a basic life-sustaining gift.
- Giving thanks before each meal.
- Following the Ten Commandments and the guidelines for doing God's will.
- Giving to charities.
- Forgiving yourself.
- Forgiving others.
- Helping another
- Setting a good example.
- Teaching the good especially to children.
- Trusting in God.

After reading the list, say the Lord's Prayer and see if there is a correlation between the acts of living the Prayer and the words of saying it. If you do not do all the above acts doing any, even one, is living the Lord's Prayer.

People have added the word amen to end the prayer. According to the dictionary, amen means: to express solemn ratification or hearty approval.[7] It is fine to say amen, it is a good word, but it is just a word. The true amen is to put the Lord's Prayer into action by living it.

Chapter 14

Prescription For Peace

Peace in the dictionary is defined as: the absence of hostilities as war, an agreement ending hostilities, a state of harmony as between persons, a state of security under the law, freedom from disquieting feelings and thoughts.[8]

This chapter could end at this point by saying that if we all lived the Lord's Prayer the above would come about but this is not our reality. There are still many false gods who by assent, or force, or ignorance control the lives of those devoted to them. There has been, is, and will be, rejection of the truth, love, and good as expressed in the Lord's Prayer. Human nature being what it is has to struggle with forces and events both within and without that disrupt peace. The Lord's Prayer is a prescription for treating those forces by offering and restoring peace. How can it do this?

How can a Prayer lead to the absence of hostilities, harmony between persons, security under the law, and freedom from disquieting thoughts? How can just words change harmful, primitive ways of thinking and relating? How can an instrument of good combat the guns and bombs of evil? It begins with ourselves. It begins with individual peace. Using the Prayer to develop individual peace is a first step. How is this step taken? Saying and living the Lord's Prayer is the start.

There is a sense of security and comfort of mind in truly believing in a Higher Power that helps us with our problems. Trusting in the love and care of the True God brings truth, love, and good into our personal realm. It also provides us with a direction in living. This direction, built on faith and trust, can help us not to be excessively worried, anxious, or fearful about living our lives. Do not be afraid is an underlying message of the Lord's Prayer.

The faith that there is life hereafter –"Thy kingdom come," that there is a heaven we can attain, that our spirit lives on, can be reassuring. It counters the disturbing thought that when we die we cease and return to darkness. That is a thought we do not like to be aware of. It can be frightening. Faith and trust in God puts death in a more comforting perspective.

Confronting stressful and troublesome issues between family and neighbor can help reduce and may eliminate the anger and tension that these type issues build up in our body systems. Why is reducing anger and anxiety important and how does it help us? Pent up anger can cause headaches, high blood pressure, heart ailments, skin conditions, accidents, fighting, broken bones, self inflicted injuries, alcohol and drug abuse. Unburdening anger helps us to live more peacefully and longer. Learning to forgive and love yourself and your neighbor can help unburden that anger.

Excessive worry, anxiety, and fear, can cause headaches, chest pain, dyspepsia (indigestion, heartburn), irritable bowel symptoms (abdominal cramping, diarrhea), fatigue, insomnia, alcohol and drug abuse. Reducing anxiety and worry helps to calm the stress on our minds and bodies. The Lord's Prayer, by helping us deal with anger and anxiety, is good medicine for our physical and mental health. Good health contributes to peace of mind.

Peace can come from doing good for others, providing for our family, teaching the children, giving to charities, caring for those in need. It has been termed the peace of mind that comes from helping another human in some way. It makes us feel good and is derived from an underlying realization that we are helping our sisters, brothers, mothers and fathers: our own human family. Where there is starvation or poverty, sharing our daily bread, our fruits, vegetables, meats, and fish is providing for the health needs of others. It contributes to peace of mind for those that receive and for those that provide. The Lord's Prayer is the format for how to help the human family, how to offer peace.

Peace of mind also comes from focusing and living in the present, the here and now, not worrying about or trying to dwell in the past or future. Focusing our attention on present interests, events, and good works, both stimulates and puts our mind at ease. Peace also comes from really seeing God's creation, which is to see its design, beauty, and purpose, and to be glad and enjoy it in the now. Peace of mind is not the same as happiness. Happiness is not what we do but being content with what we are doing. Happiness will contribute to peace of mind if the doing involves truth, love, and good.

We have already discussed how destructive and troublesome to our well being evil is. There is no need to elaborate further on this; just look at what believing in false gods, deceiving, killing, war, rape, greed, have brought upon the human race throughout our history. There is no peace in evil. There is grief, torment, anguish, and despair. "Deliver us from evil" is a request to lead us to peace. Delivering each other from evil is an action towards providing peace.

Summarizing at this point, individual peace of mind consists of: living in truth, focusing in the present, being in the reality of our current condition or situation, dealing with issues that need to be confronted, reducing or eliminating anger and fear in our system, taking care of ourselves and others, seeing the plan and beauty in creation, and having trust in God's higher power.

Peace on earth begins with individual peace as summarized above and extends through our immediate family out into relationships with others. Peace with others includes seeing them sharing existence as members of our human family. It is a peace that speaks to strangers, to those who are different. It is a peace that forgives those who trespass against us. It is a peace that provides truth, love, and good to all peoples: a peace that reaches ultimately to nations.

Love God, love your neighbor, and love yourself is the message of the Lord's Prayer. What can provide more harmony and peace among people than that? So, it is important for us to live the Lord's Prayer, for to do so is to contribute toward the final goal of peace on earth as it is in heaven.

Chapter 15

Why Were We Given The Lord's Prayer

A thoughtful, important question: one that requires reflection and is a fitting close to this book. In reviewing the chapters many of the reasons we were given the Lord's Prayer have already been expressed; however, they need to be looked at within the context of the question – why? Why did this prayer come forth on earth in the time and place that it did? Like discovery, was there a need in waiting for those words of God to become apparent to us?

The Prayer is a summary of the word, will, and message of God. It contains the story of the Old Testament, the guidelines of the New Testament, defines a True God, and sends us the message to forgive and love each other: quite a package contained in just fifty-five words. Truly it is a gift to humanity meant to be delivered to each of us. But, why was it necessary? Since nothing in the Lord's Prayer is without purpose, the following thoughts are an attempt to understand why we were given this particular prayer.

The main working concept that the Prayer brings to us is forgiveness. Forgiveness is central to its teachings. It is the only directive given in the Prayer: be forgiven as you forgive. Why is forgiveness of such value as to be delivered emphatically and directly to us by the word of God?

Prior to the Lord's Prayer and during the age it appeared many of the varied human populations based their empires, kingdoms, and thinking on conquer or slaughter, subjugate and rule. Hordes and armies, tribes and legions had swept back and forth over the world killing, plundering, destroying, capturing, and enslaving. This becomes apparent when reviewing world history including the history of the Bible. In fact the Bible begins with one brother murdering another and ends with a murder carried out under Roman rule. Apart from the good in the momentums (life, reproduction, and discovery), our history has been of human beings fighting and destroying each other. It has been of war, conquest or defeat, of untold numbers of youths killing themselves and others.

A war-like and revengeful society did not think in terms of forgiveness and love of neighbor. Those concepts either did not exist or if present were ignored or suppressed. People lived in uncertainty and fear of an enemy. Towns and cities were built on mountain-sides or surrounded by walls, forts, and moats to protect against invasion. Then, into our embattled history came a prayer – the Lord's Prayer – with words presenting a diametrically opposite way of thinking about, dealing with, and relating to others, including the enemy – forgive and love them. This prayer was a vehicle that brought the concept of forgiveness and the message of love your neighbor into the mind of humanity. It presented a different order of thinking.

Most likely there were elements of forgiveness in ancient religions, teachings, and philosophies; as forgiveness is an innate expression present in children towards their parents; however, it can get submerged under hurt feelings, anger, resentment, hate, revenge, and fear. Not harming or killing any type of life was and is a practice based on a belief in reincarnation and respect for life. Meditation was and is the seeking of inner peace. These practices are of value to their adherents and may contain aspects of forgiveness. The Israelites sought God's forgiveness through atonement by ritualistic animal sacrifice. However, the forgiveness that the Lord's Prayer speaks to – the act of love towards neighbor – was expressed when the Author of the Prayer, while being nailed to a cross said, "Father forgive them, they know not what they do." At that point an old attitude met the new order.

The hordes and tribes, Huns, Vandals, and barbarians have passed, most of the militant empires are gone, most of the warlords and schemers who led countries into battle in order to conquer or annihilate others have been defeated; yet, the concepts of forgiveness and love of neighbor still stand strong. The people of history who have acted within these concepts have shown us their value: a testimony to the power of their truths, a better way of life, and the means to the common good.

The Lord's Prayer appeared in the 30's A.D. during the spread of the Roman Empire. This extensive empire, based on conquer and subjugate, reached from England (Britannia) across Europe, through Turkey (Asia Minor) to Armenia and Iraq (Mesopotamia), down over Syria and Israel and across Egypt and northern Africa (Carthage). It was a pagan society in that its subjects worshiped multiple mythologic gods, their statues, and temples. The emperor was designated a divinity – a god. The Roman Army was the most formidable fighting force of the time spreading the empire and its religion over the adjacent world.

The pagan Roman onslaught had to be a threat to the belief in a one true God, the knowledge of

Whom was being kept alive by a relatively small society of conquered people, the Jews, living in the hills of Judea; whose own faith was at risk under Roman rule. The only way that this threat of misguiding humanity could be met head on without violence was through a prayer: a prayer that offered peace. Thus, entered the Lord's Prayer and just in time as the Romans destroyed Jerusalem and the temple of the Jewish God in 70A.D.

The Lord's Prayer brought God down from the sky, from the sun, out of the forests, out of the stones and statues, into our bodies: into our minds and our hearts. We were originally told to say the Prayer in secret, in the privacy of our room: in so doing we became the temple of the Word with its force and mission. Thus, God was able to work through us so that the new order concepts of forgiveness and love of neighbor could take effect. The teachings of the Lord's Prayer began to spread within humanity and ironically it was the Roman roads and waterways that facilitated its spread.

All roads lead to Rome was the saying of that age as the Romans had built a system of ways and trails through their conquered lands; a main purpose being so that the legions could depart and return with their booty and captives to enhance the wealth and work-force of Rome. The roads also facilitated travel and communication so an edict, a Roman law, levied taxes, or a new concept could be communicated quicker and further. The infrastructure was in place providing the way for the Lord's Prayer to be brought to the people; the word of forgiveness and love was also on the march, heading towards Rome itself.

The power of the Lord's Prayer was released throughout the Roman Empire by believing in the Prayer: believing in a one true God – "Hallowed be Thy Name," believing in a kingdom of God with a willingness to die for the kingdom – martyrdom – "Thy kingdom come." The power of the Prayer was spread by doing the will of God – "Thy will be done": forgiving the enemy, the persecutor, the executioner. The power of the Prayer was spread by living it, setting the good example, and trusting in God uncompromisingly. Saying the Prayer together fostered community and with community much becomes possible: in this case the conversion of Rome.

At the time, widely spoken Greek was the language of culture and scholars; Latin was the language of the law of the land, the language of Rome. Into these universal languages entered the words of the Prayer. From its local origin, possibly a small village or a hillside, it spread around the Mediterranean region and then radiated out into the rest of the adjacent world. The new order was being conveyed. The fact that this message of forgive and love others was received, accepted, and then passed on by people in widely spaced geographic areas, showed that a need for it was waiting; a receptive audience was present. But, what was the need that the Lord's Prayer resonated with and responded to?

We have noted that the belief in a one true God was in danger of being extinguished and replaced by the multiple false gods of Rome. If so, this had to be a threat to the awareness of the true God's presence on earth. Throughout Biblical history, God has intervened whenever humanity reached a critical point in drifting away from the truth. When the Ten Commandments were given to us the Israelites were bowing to a golden calf, symbolic of idolatry and worship of riches (gold). Likewise the Lord's Prayer came into our awareness when much of the world was practicing idolatry and worshiping riches. The coming of the Lord's Prayer was an intervention to refocus humanity.

At the time the Prayer appeared there had been much suffering on earth. As a result of conquest, people were enslaved to toil, be abused, and to die at the hands of their overlords. Freedom of thought and expression was curtailed. Again, history gives us insight: the Israelites were delivered from slavery so they could worship unencumbered their one true God. The Lord's Prayer was and still is a deliverance from slavery – slavery of the mind. It can be said anywhere and under all circumstances: from home, to field, to prison. It requires no temple, statue, or priest. It was and is a direct communication to God.

To the blind, the lame, the diseased, the poor, the homeless, the outcasts, to all who were suffering mentally and physically, the Lord's Prayer brought consolation and hope. But, it brought more than hope: it paved the way for humanity to be able to work together, to show love of neighbor, to discover medicines, to alleviate pain, to restore vision, to build hospitals, to provide for the poor and homeless. The Lord's Prayer in itself was a miracle and still is.

Prior to the coming of the Prayer, there were people waiting for the word of God to appear on earth. The prophets and wisemen of old give document to this. The expectation of a Messiah is another example. There were scattered religious and non-religious groups hoping and praying for God to help them. The intelligent thinkers of Rome and Greece were becoming aware of the futility in worshiping stone statues and mythology: as shown by their leaders eventually embracing the teaching of the Prayer. The Lord's Prayer was an answer to those who were waiting, those who could hear it, those who could believe it, those who needed it. And, more than an answer to needs, the Prayer gave us a blueprint for living life as a civilized community.

When the Lord's Prayer appeared on earth it was a crucial time for the word of the true God to confront the spread of false belief. It was a time of relatively advanced development in roads and communication. It was a time when much of humanity lived in fear of an enemy or under the dominance of a conqueror. It was a time when the poor, sick, and suffering needed help. It was a time when the learned and others were looking towards a new kingdom on earth. The timing was right for, and it was necessary for, this Prayer to enter humanity.

Did accepting and living the principles inherent in the Lord's Prayer facilitate discovery? An important consideration approached by looking at some major discoveries since the origin of the Prayer and noting if their use was concordant with its intentions (of the Prayer); in other words did they benefit humanity? Since the coming of the Lord's Prayer we have discovered:

automobiles which improved transportation and led to the ambulance, fire, and rescue trucks - which save lives

airplanes and helicopters used for rescue and medivacs

railroads and subway systems for ease of travel especially for the young, handicapped, and elderly

electricity for use of the lightbulb, the heater, elevators, and respirators

telephones (911)

television and computers

the x-ray machine, the M.R.I.

open heart, coronary bypass and vascular surgery

the cotton gin, the grain harvester, the tractor for farming

trucks for transporting our necessities

The above list indeed shows major discoveries that have helped improve the human condition considerably. It is interesting to note that the potential for the above discoveries existed long before the discoveries took place. As examples:

The wheel, fire, metal, and math existed for thousands of years but it was not until after the

Lord's Prayer came on earth that an automotive vehicle with an internal combustion engine was discovered. Electricity was always present and humans watched birds fly overhead for centuries, but it was not until after the Lord's Prayer that electricity was discovered to be used and people began to fly long distances like the birds. Human beings labored harvesting grain by hand with scythe and sickle for thousands of years but it was not until after the Lord's Prayer that the mechanical grain reaper was discovered. How long did human-kind plow its fields by hand and foot and horse until the tractor came into being?

As mentioned before there seems to be a time and purpose for discovery to take place. The ancient sciences, astronomy and mathematics, existing for eons, lay in waiting like the fossil fuels until the thinking was ready for their application to be of benefit to people everywhere. Pyramids and chariots did not improve the plight of humanity. They were used for burying the select few and for battles and races. Ancient technical advances were utilized for making weapons such as spears, swords, and armor, or for building fortresses, statues, temples, and palaces: uses primarily for fighting, killing, protection, and worshiping false gods – a reflection of the old way of thinking.

If advanced weaponry and atomic energy as exists today were discovered before the message of the Lord's Prayer was accepted by human-kind, they would have been used under the old way of thinking for conquest or annihilation and still could be used that way under that type of attitude. Discovery appears to come when humanity is receptive to a peaceful option for its use; thus fulfilling its God given purpose.

From its individuals, nations can show forgiveness. After World War ll, instead of reverting to the old way of revenge, domination, and enslavement, the allied countries freed, fed, financially supported, and fostered the rebuilding of the German and Japanese economy. Look at the Marshal Plan (European Recovery Program) that provided aid, food, and money (16.5 billion) to a devastated Europe. Learn about the allied ships that transported Japanese soldiers back to their homeland to be with their families. These were acts of forgive and love your neighbor; in this case the enemy. The new order of thinking and acting was being carried out. As a result look at what post war Germany and Japan have been able to do for their people, for their economy, and to contribute to the world.

Note that all the previous listed discoveries occurred in countries that had accepted the Lord's Prayer and allowed its citizens to pray and live it. Is this just coincidence or does it reflect an answer to the section prayer – "give us this day our daily bread"? Remember, our daily bread includes all that we have and all that improves our quality of life.

In the Prayer the phrase connected to "give us this day our daily bread" is "and forgive us our trespasses as we forgive those who trespass against us." Did the new order of thinking with forgiveness instead of retaliation, love instead of hate, bring forth the beneficial discoveries that we utilize today? The connection between daily bread and forgiveness in the Lord's Prayer appears to indicate so. These discoveries were not only of benefit to people in countries embracing the Lord's Prayer, they were meant for people everywhere and have been of use all over the world. They are for the good of human-kind.

Yellow fever, malaria, cholera, smallpox, tuberculosis, sepsis ravaged humanity until their causes were discovered: relatively recent in the span of human existence. Through the thinking and effect of health research, of human service organizations, and caregivers helping their neighbors – living the Lord's Prayer – most of those diseases have been eradicated in many parts of the world. If the Lord's Prayer did not facilitate discovery per se, it influenced the use of discovery for the benefit of others – an act of love. Think about the ambulance. Think about the tractor.

The idea of the Lord's Prayer enhancing or influencing the good use of discovery is in keeping with the mission of the Prayer: to love God, your neighbor, and yourself. It suggests that discoveries of benefit to humanity can have far reaching, even currently unknown achievements, such as: all diseases and illness being eradicated, all peoples being fed, life being prolonged, natural catastrophes being averted; sorrow would decline, world peace could be achieved. The sky's the limit. To enhance beneficial discovery may be a major reason why we were given the Lord's Prayer.

Another form of discovery has been the development of a democratic system of living: a system in which there is freedom of vitality, freedom of speech, freedom of education, freedom to elect officials, freedom from slavery, freedom of religion, and freedom to discover; a system in which people can share life, liberty, and the pursuit of happiness, and govern with unity for the common good.

Prayer is symbolic of freedom of self expression and freedom of self expression initiates discovery. It is people like us saying and living the Lord's Prayer that bring out its benefits. A government can be atheistic but that does not mean its citizens are not praying. During World War II good people on both sides were praying the Lord's Prayer asking for an end to the war and a defeat of its evils: which ultimately took place.

The blending within the Prayer of the Old and New Testaments shows that they are connected and as we have noted the Lord's Prayer is the transition between them. But what is the lesson in this for us now in our present day? It can be summed up in one word – unity: the bringing together and joining together for a common purpose. The merging of the old story and the new news conveys the spirit of unity. Their convergence is unity. The message to love God, love your neighbor, and love yourself is the means to unity: the unity of the Lord's Prayer that utilizes the knowledge and help of the true God to join together all individuals, all families, and all nations for the common good and well being of the human race.

Well, these are some of my thoughts on why we were given the Lord's Prayer. I am sure there are more reasons. The more you think about the Prayer the more it reveals. If God did not have a plan for us we would not have a Lord's Prayer. Its very existence is a document to this plan. Adding your thoughts on why we were given this Prayer, either in the secret room of your mind or in the public forum, would be the best way to complete this passage and move on to continue your journey. The Lord's Prayer is a beginning; we (us) are the end.

Glossary

All good: perfect love as shown in creation, in providing our daily bread, in forgiveness, and in giving us the Lord's Prayer.

Evil: the willful rejection of the true God in a way that is manifest by the worship of false gods. Doing the opposite of God's will.

False gods: persons, places, and things that become a priority to the exclusion of the true God.

Forgive: to stop being angry or resentful towards another and to love those who have trespassed against us.

Hallowed: to honor as morally and spiritually perfect or all good.

Heaven: where God is, a place or state of truth, love, and all good.

Intelligent design: a plan and purpose for and in creation.

Living the Lord's Prayer: putting the intentions of the Prayer into action.

Lord's Prayer: the love, intentions, and message, of the true God.

Love of Enemy: to will good and do good to those who trespass against us, highest level of forgiveness.

Love of God: to believe in and focus one's trust upon the true God, to do the will of God, to live the Lord's Prayer.

Love of Neighbor: to will good and do good for another.

Love of Self: to will good and do good to yourself.

Message of the Prayer: love God, love your neighbor, and love yourself.

Our Daily Bread: all that keeps us alive, that nourishes our mind and body, that improves our quality of life, including food for thought and creativity, and the Word of God.

Our Father: opening words of the Lord's Prayer recognizing God as a good father and creator of all. Identifies a true God.

Peace (individual): living the truth, being in the present, confronting the issue, loving self and others, seeing intelligent design, trusting in the true God.

Peace on earth: a peace that provides truth, love, and good, to all peoples.

Personal intention: to say the Lord's Prayer with love for self, another person, event, or to give thanks.

Secret room: a quiet place in our home, a secret place in our mind.

Temptation: any thing that would lead us to not want to do the will of God.

This day: the present, the here and now, where our current existence is.

Thy Kingdom: the result of the assembly of those who do or have done the will of the true God and whose trespasses have been forgiven.

Trespass: to violate God's will in a way that affects another person.

true God (small t): a God who is not a false god, identified in the Lord's Prayer as Our Father.

True God (capital T): the God revealed through the Lord's Prayer, whose essence is the power of truth, love, and all good.

Truth: is what really is, also the word of the true God.

Us: the word that connects us to God and to each other. It implies that we share in doing God's will on earth.

Will of God: guidelines for good living given to us by God as the Ten Commandments and the life and words of Jesus Christ.

References

[1,4,6,8] Definitions of create, vain, forgive, peace: "Copyright © 2008 by Houghton Mifflin Harcourt Publishing Company. Reproduced by permission from Webster's New College Dictionary, Third Edition."

[2,3,5,7] Definitions of kingdom, will, trespass, amen: "By permission from the Merriam-Webster Online Dictionary © 2009 by Merriam-Webster, Incorporated (www.Merriam-Webster.com)."

The Author

Tony Chatowsky is a retired psychiatrist who was called Dr. C by his patients and co-workers. He attended college in Rhode Island, medical school in New York City, interned in Portland, Oregon, took his psychiatric training in Topeka, Kansas, and currently lives in Florida.

LaVergne, TN USA
31 October 2010
202941LV00002B/1/P